THE NEW SOCIAL WORK

JUSTICE AND THE LAW
IN THE MOBILIZATION FOR YOUTH EXPERIENCE

Justice and the Law

in the Mobilization
for Youth Experience

EDITED BY HAROLD H. WEISSMAN

ASSOCIATION PRESS   NEW YORK

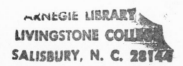

JUSTICE AND THE LAW IN THE MOBILIZATION FOR YOUTH EXPERIENCE

Copyright © 1969 by
National Board of Young Men's Christian Associations

Association Press, 291 Broadway, New York, N. Y. 10007

SBN: Hardbound edition 8096-1729-3
Paperback edition   8096-1734-X

Library of Congress catalog card number: 69-18846

PRINTED IN THE UNITED STATES OF AMERICA

TO
WINSLOW CARLTON
Chairman of the Board
Mobilization For Youth

For Dedication and Devotion
to the Objectives of
the Program

Preface

At its founding, there were several program aspects which distinguished Mobilization For Youth from other social agencies. One was that Mobilization allocated a sizable portion of its resources to research. Yet even with these substantial resources, research could not concern itself with all of the agency's programs. Decisions as to priorities were based on the projected effectiveness of various programs, their relation to the theory which provided the foundation for the overall project, and whether the programs could conform to the rigors of research methodology without compromising either their quality or purpose.

Some programs were researched in great detail; others, only in relation to specific aspects; and some, unfortunately, had to be left uninvestigated.[1] By early 1965, it was clear that much of the experience of the agency would be lost unless it was systematically described and analyzed.

Of particular concern was the practice knowledge that had been gained—the reservoir of insights, ideas, experiences, and judgments about the range of interaction and interventions staff were involved in, the structures and mechanisms they had devised, and the results achieved through their efforts.

To codify and refine this practice knowledge, MFY applied for a grant from the Office of Juvenile Delinquency and Youth Development of the Department of Health, Education and Welfare.

[1] A list of the research studies and reports produced at Mobilization is appended to this volume. In addition an epilogue and a discussion of the administration of the total MFY program follow the papers on legal services.

7

Grant No. 67224, effective July 1, 1966, through June 30, 1968, provided for a Program Reporting Department consisting of a staff of writers and program analysts. According to the grant's stipulations, the department was to . . .

. . . tell the story of each program division from its beginning, inserting at the appropriate places changes or new emphases divergent from those originally conceived, problems which emerged during the course of the program and how they were dealt with, techniques and methods which were used successfully and unsuccessfully, involvement with other MFY programs, participation statistics as well as any other pertinent statistical information. It will also include descriptions of program accomplishments, and other useful information relating to aspects of the program such as training and hiring of staff, administration and supervision. The intention . . . is to provide people who have participated in a unique social adventure with an opportunity to develop their own ideas and practice insights and to exchange them with others similarly engaged.

A few of the papers which appear in this book and the other volumes in this collection were written by line staff members of the particular divisions; most were written by the Program Reporting staff; some are an amalgam of the work of both line staff and Program Reporting staff. A member of the Program Reporting staff was assigned responsibility for the reports on each of the program divisions of Mobilization. This responsibility included gathering all prior reports and published material of the division, developing with line staff an outline for the projected volume, observing the operation of programs, preparing working drafts—alone or in conjunction with line staff—and discussing these with all staff involved with the topic being covered.

All the papers in this volume went through several drafts; many were substantially altered, some were combined, and some, after discussion with the staff, were omitted. Michael Appleby gathered most of the data and wrote initial drafts of the papers as part of his doctoral dissertation at the Massachusetts Institute of Technology.

Henry Heifetz and I revised these papers to fit the purposes of this volume.

As editor, it was my responsibility to make final decisions as to what material should be included, what should be emphasized, and what value should be accorded various conflicting ideas and sentiments. In this process any bias or error which inadvertently crept in remains my responsibility.

There are a great many able people to whom considerable credit is due; foremost is Bertram M. Beck, executive director of Mobilization since 1965. He first conceived the idea for these volumes and was instrumental in obtaining the grant that made them possible. Harold Rothwax, director of the Division of Legal Services and Dr. Richard Cloward former director of research of MFY read drafts of the papers and made helpful comments and suggestions.

Danielle Spellman, Nancy Dannenberg, and Martha King typed and retyped the papers, not without complaint but always with humor and concern. Each of them also, when the need arose, assisted in observing programs and were helpful critics of the papers. Jeannette Heinbach carried on for them during the final editorial stages and was similarly helpful.

Beverly Luther served as my assistant in this project. Without her help it could not have been brought to a conclusion. She relieved me of a variety of administrative duties and faultlessly followed through with innumerable details. Gladys Topkis edited the papers, as she has done with so much of the written material produced at Mobilization. A considerable portion of the credit for the style and clarity of the material goes to her.

This book and each of the other three volumes—*Individual and Group Services, Community Development, Employment and Educational Services*—begin with a statement of the ideas and concepts the workers intended to apply in a particular program division. The individual chapters which make up each volume describe what happened when these ideas were put into effect and what was learned from the experience. Some of the chapters deal with the history of a specific program, some deal with broad issues and concerns in social work and other professions, and others describe experiences in many programs. The concluding chapter in each section summarizes the major issues which emerged from the experiences described.

The four volumes are meant to constitute an intellectual history of a project which in all likelihood represents a watershed in the development of social welfare in America. This type of history perforce emphasizes learning. It does not tell the comprehensive history of the agency. It may even dwell more on failures than prudent public relations would dictate. The volumes, as such, are not intended to provide a balanced picture of the agency. They are intended, rather, to give readers an opportunity to share the insights, ideas, experiences, and judgments of those who shaped and were shaped by it.

—H. H. W.

Contents

11

        Bertram M. Beck

10. Politics and Planning: Mobilization as a Model   167
        Frances Fox Piven

    Epilogue   192
        Harold H. Weissman

    Appendices

    1. Index of Research Studies   205
            Richard A. Cloward

    2. Board of Directors   215

    Index   217

THE NEW SOCIAL WORK

JUSTICE AND THE LAW
IN THE MOBILIZATION FOR YOUTH EXPERIENCE

Introduction

The slum is, in its least complex form, a disorderly mechanism for human destruction, operating through crumbling houses and relatively unconnected inhabitants in a loosely defined geographic area. At its most developed, it is a homeland for a particular minority group or assemblage of groups, a neighborhood with its own traditions, where a foreign language may be the common tongue and where the accepted customs, loyalties, and hostilities may be divergent from, or even directly opposed to, those of society outside. New York City encompasses a wide assortment of slums, of all sizes and conditions, in all stages of development and disorder. Among them, Manhattan's Lower East Side has the longest history as a slum neighborhood, although the component languages and customs have changed several times through the years and are not uniform today from one group's heartland in the area to another's.

The Lower East Side first became a slum neighborhood thanks very largely to the Irish Potato Famine of 1846, which drove the impoverished "wild geese" abroad as mercenaries and refugees. Irish immigrants began to pour into America in the 1840's and 1850's. New York received a larger number than any other city and several parts of the Lower East Side became Irish homelands, especially the Five Points area, where a small Irish enclave still exists, and the area along the East River, where many Irish were employed on the docks. The zone near the Bowery became a drinking and red-light district. Like later minority groups who felt themselves isolated by poverty in the middle of the New Paradise they had come to find, the Irish formed gangs. The famous Bowery Gangs included both adults and adolescents and controlled their "turf" with savagery. And, as was true of later delinquent and gangster groups, the Irish proved to be useful to the powers-that-be—in this case Tammany Hall—who found employment for the Irish Bowery Gangs during elections, and a value in the Irish vote.

Then the Irish took over Tammany Hall and became American, through the acquisition of political power and the process of acculturation. They were fortunate in that this process for them did not involve learning a foreign language or accepting a basically alien culture. In the eyes of some of the groups that succeeded them on the Lower East Side, the image of the American was that of the Irishman.

The Germans began arriving in the 1860's and 1870's and became for a time the most numerous immigrant group in the city. In the 1860's it was estimated that two thirds of the 120,000 German-born residents of New York City lived on the Lower East Side in an area which the immigrants called *Kleindeutschland,* or *Deutschlandle.* Many of the Irish moved away, and the beer halls and delicatessens of Germany were duplicated on the streets of the Lower East Side.

This German Lower East Side seems to have been a comparatively peaceful slum. Many of the immigrants were artisans. There were fewer peasants than among the Irish, and big city living, in their recreated Germany, seems to have come fairly easily to them. The Germans, even given the handicap of their foreign language, were a group whose customs, tastes, and personal appearance did not militate against their relatively undramatic integration into American society.

This was not the case with the next two immigrant groups to arrive in the Lower East Side. The eastern European Jews and the primarily southern Italians who came in hordes toward the end of the nineteenth century were foreign in their customs, looks, and language, with a tendency to shout and laugh in public too loudly for the taste of traditional America, surrounded with the aura of sensuality and depravity with which lighter-skinned races have always tended to endow those darker than themselves.

The center of Little Italy lay west of the Lower East Side, but the Italian population extended well into the area. The immigrants were almost all peasants or else refugees from the hideous slums of Naples and Palermo and Agrigento. They came to America in swaying ships packed with hundreds of their fellows, and were met by waiting relatives who took them to the tenements that would be their new homes. The tubs of family washing and the piles of sewing to be done on a piecework basis might already be prepared for the girl, the address of the gang-labor contractor and his assurances of "plenty of work for a boy from the old hometown" welcomed the man. They constructed their Little Italy as well as they could, but for a Sicilian peasant, the sidewalks of New York buried in snow differed in more than geography and climate from the sun-baked, rocky farmlands of Sicily. The southern Italian came from a region of feudal landlords who were still called barons, an intensely traditional and immovable society; in America everything seemed in flux and up for grabs, provided that one was ruthless or knowledgeable enough. Those who were not, struggled along; those who were rose out of areas like the Lower East Side into the goods and benefits of middle-class American living, through the routes of business, politics, dogged and desperate acquisition of a professional education, or crime. For some there was a bitter price to be paid in renunciation, in self-hatred for the foreignness which the parents had given and the child still, in spite of himself, retained. American acceptability often came at a profound psychological cost.

The eastern European Jews were the group that most characterized the Lower East Side in the first half of the twentieth century. In New York, in the nation at large, and outside America, the Lower East Side came to mean the Jewish ghetto. By 1900, the East Side was already the largest, most densely populated Jewish community in the world. Of two million Jewish immigrants in America at the time of World War I, three quarters had lived for a time on the Lower East Side. Although there remained scattered pockets of other ethnic groups—Italians, a handful of Germans, small neighborhoods of Irish, an enclave of Slavonic people—virtually all of the Lower East Side, from Cherry Street to Tenth Street, from the East River to the Bowery, was considered the ghetto.

The Russian pogroms of the 1880's and 1890's were the propelling force for the Jewish immigration. There had been a settlement of German Jews on the Lower East Side before then, and these now Americanized Germans tended to be ill at ease with their alien coreligionists, condescending and superior. Some of them owned the garment businesses in which the new arrivals were employed. Other German Jews were active in philanthropy and in attempts to Americanize the immigrants.

The East European Jews themselves were divided into groups who spoke different dialects of Yiddish and had somewhat different customs. Russians, Lithuanians, Poles, Galicians, and Romanians tended to settle among their own and preserve their own cultural variants, but they could easily understand each other's Yiddish. The Lower East Side became a center of Yiddish culture, with a developed literature, an extremely active theater, and six flourishing newspapers, including the still existing *Daily Forward*. In its time, the *Forward* was an important Socialist newspaper, in the forefront of the Jewish labor movement during the days of the early unions and the violent strikes.

The Jewish East Side has become known, through the writings of nostalgic former residents, as a foreign enclave, with foods and sounds and colors and customs that marked it apart from the larger society. It was that, of course, but it was also a tenement slum where the measure of success was departure, where the young members of street gangs fought and developed into full-time hoodlums struggling with the Irish and Italian gangsters for the vast spoils of Prohibition.

America's first settlement house, the University Settlement, was founded on the Lower East Side in the 1880's. The settlement movement on the Lower East Side pioneered in attempts to deal with the problems of slums, such as campaigns for increased recreational facilities, housing reform, and child-labor legislation.

In the 1930's and 1940's the ghetto began to break up. Many Jews moved to the Bronx and Brooklyn, leaving behind the old, the economically trapped, and the failures. In the next two decades another group of immigrants arrived to change once again the complexion and language of the Lower East Side. Puerto Ricans have come in vast numbers from the slums of Ponce and San Juan and New York's East Harlem, joined by lesser number of Negroes from the American South or from New York's Harlem or Bedford-Stuyvesant. The combined Negro and Puerto Rican population of New York City increased 250 percent between 1925 and 1950. A small colony of Puerto Rican cigarmakers had lived on Cherry Street in the Lower East Side since the 1920's, but the major destination of the postwar Puerto Rican immigration to New York City was "El Barrio," East Harlem centering around Third Avenue and 101st Street. The Negroes coming up from the South and the West Indies went first to Harlem and later to Bedford-Stuyvesant, which were long-established Negro ghettos. Therefore, for the Puerto Ricans and Negroes who began moving down to the Lower East Side in the 1940's and 1950's as the Jewish population vacated the tenements, the Lower East Side was not a primary area of settlement, a homeland, as it had been for the Germans and the Jews, but a spillover area without structure or traditions.

Many of the tenement streets awaiting the newcomers were little different from what they had been fifty or sixty years before, but the postwar building boom had swept some of the others away. Low-income public housing projects and middle-income cooperatives have been built on the Lower East Side. The cooperatives have brought the middle class into the neighborhood for the first time in a century, to join the low-income Puerto Ricans and Negroes who live in the tenements and public housing projects. The residents of the cooperatives are generally middle class or so-called stable working class whites, primarily Jewish. In the tenements east of Avenue B, the western boundary of the Mobilization For Youth project, almost none of the previous white residents remain. In recent years increasing, though still relatively small numbers of a different kind of slum dweller have arrived: artists and those who attach themselves to artistic communities, drawn by the low rents growing less and less available in Greenwich Village. In the parlance of renting agents, the Lower East Side is now the East Village, as a result of this movement and in the attempt to capitalize on it.

The section of the Lower East Side which Mobilization For Youth singled out as its target area is primarily a Puerto Rican slum. Some Italians still live in the southern portion, a small Slavonic group to the north, a number of Chinese on certain streets who are moving over from Chinatown to the west. Jews still own much of the housing and many of the businesses, and there are old-fashioned outdoor Jewish markets on Orchard Street and on Avenue C. From a survey of the Mobilization area taken in 1961, it was estimated that 27 percent of the population was Jewish, most of them residents of the cooperatives. But the basically Puerto Rican nature of the area is very evident from the record shops and bodegas and botanicas and the bongos out on the street at the first touch of spring.

The postwar wave of Puerto Rican immigration now seems to be nearing its end. The Puerto Ricans came, as citizens of the United States, for the economic opportunities which were wanting in Puerto Rico, and they stayed because, even in the rat-ridden tenements of El Barrio, things really were somewhat better here, or at least more promising.

New York offered many of the Puerto Ricans their first confrontation with direct racial prejudice. The pecking order of the oppressed tended to establish itself again as in America it usually, sadly has. A certain degree of hostility developed between Negroes and Puerto Ricans since they were competing for the same bottom-of-the-heap jobs and some of the same slum housing, and, less materially, because the bottom of society is a very narrow place for people to share. Recognizable Negro–Puerto Ricans, a minority among the immigrants, were in a very difficult position: On the one hand they had to deal with a double load of prejudice; on the other, many of them came to feel that being Spanish and black was somehow better than being simply an American Negro, and so they clung even more tenaciously to their language and denied all connection with the American black man. On occasion, as occurred in the process of rent-strike organizing activities on the Lower East Side, light-skinned Puerto Ricans have been told they were "more American" than the darker-skinned Hispanicos and used as a shock force against their own people.

Gradually that section of the Lower East Side which forms the Mobilization For Youth project area is becoming the kind of slum one can call a neighborhood. The Puerto Rican has come to feel at home in the Lower East Side, and the area has become a zone of "Spanish color." But even a slum that is a neighborhood continued to be a machine for human destruction. The difficulties with school that usually burden lower-class youngsters are multiplied for children whose native language is Spanish and whose cultural values are Caribbean. During the late 1950's, the "heroic era" of teenage gang warfare in New York City, some of the casualties took place on the Lower East Side where bopping gangs formed by kids of Puerto Rican, Italian and Negro descent fought with adult weapons for control of their respective turf. With the decline of the conflict gangs, and in part a reason for the decline, came a huge increase in heroin addiction throughout New York. The junkie on the nod as the result of a shot of horse became an everyday sight on the Lower East Side. And many of the junkies were adolescents, copping out young on the consumer's society that seemed to have very little in the way of possible consumption to offer them.

Along with the increase in addiction came an upsurge in petty theft. Slum dwellers are always the first to suffer from those among them who choose criminal activity. This pattern of declining gang conflict and rising heroin addiction and petty crime characterized juvenile delinquency on the Lower East Side when, in 1962, Mobilization For Youth actively undertook to "mount . . . a major demonstration program to attack the problem of juvenile delinquency" by "expanding opportunities for conventional behavior."

Mobilization For Youth had its inception at a meeting of the board of directors of the Henry Street Settlement in June 1957, where a report was read on the growth of delinquency on the Lower East Side. In the Mobilization area this rate grew from 28.7 offenses per 1,000 youths in 1951 to 62.8 per 1,000 in 1960. Appalled by the dimensions of the problem, the board proposed that research begin immediately on a program of massive response to the increasing rate of juvenile delinquency. A planning process began which took four and a half years to complete. During a preliminary stage, faculty members of the Columbia University School of Social Work, assisted by a grant from the Taconic Foundation, conducted research emphasizing the existing youth-serving agencies on the Lower East Side and what could be learned from them in terms of practice. In a second stage of research, beginning in November 1959 and made possible by grants from the National Institute of Mental Health, a unifying principle of expanding opportunities was worked out as a direct basis for action. This principle was drawn from the concepts outlined by sociologists Richard Cloward and Lloyd Ohlin in their book *Delinquency and Opportunity*. Drs. Cloward and Ohlin regarded delinquency as the result of the disparity perceived by low-income youths between their legitimate aspirations and the opportunities—social, economic, political, educational—made available to them by society. If the gap between opportunity and aspiration could be bridged, they believed delinquency would be reduced; that would be the agency's goal.

The geographical boundaries set for Mobilization coincided with the zone of greatest poverty and highest delinquency on the Lower East Side: Avenue B on the west, the East River on the east, East 14th Street to the north and the City Hall junction to the south running into a tip of Lower Manhattan. The area had a population in 1961 of approximately 107,000, of whom 27 percent were Jewish, 11 percent Italian, 25 percent "other white," 8 percent Negro, 3 percent Oriental, and 26 percent Puerto Rican. These percentages do not reflect the ethnic groups served by Mobilization however, for a considerable number of the whites, as we have noted, were financially stable, with little need for Mobilization services. The youth population was 90 percent Puerto Rican and Negro.

And the percentage of Puerto Rican and Negro residents almost doubled between 1960 and 1967.

More than half of the tenement housing (62.4 percent) was classified as substandard by the 1960 census. Although the city-wide unemployment rate in that year was 5.0 percent some ninety neighborhoods (half of them in Manhattan) had rates at least twice the citywide figure. The Lower East Side contained one third of Manhattan's double-rate neighborhoods. Forty-one percent of its households received some form of financial assistance, and 37 percent of its adult residents had failed to complete the eighth grade.

A thirty-three-man board of directors was established for Mobilization, including eleven factulty members from the Columbia School of Social Work and leaders of various citywide and national agencies, such as the Office of the Commonwealth of Puerto Rico, the New York Community Service Society, and the Urban League. Major funding came from the City of New York, the National Institute of Mental Health, the Ford Foundation, and the President's Committee on Juvenile Delinquency.

Supplied with these resources and armed with its extensive background of preparation and research, Mobilization For Youth began its service projects in 1962, with a staff of about three hundred.

Besides a Division of Research, programs were grouped under four major divisions: Educational Services, Employment Services, Services to Individuals and Families, and Community Development. This latter division included Services to Groups. In 1964 a fifth division, Legal Services, was added.

The project from the first attracted much local and national attention because of the experimental nature of its programs and the prospect that, should Mobilization's modes of dealing with the problem of juvenile delinquency prove successful, similar programs might be mounted throughout the country. Many of the staff members were highly trained specialists; others were local residents who had had experience in community work; nearly all began their work with a high degree of commitment and enthusiasm. What follows is a record of their effort.

Henry Heifetz

1

Overview of Legal Services

Michael Appleby

As compared with the legal problems of the more affluent classes, those of the poor are frequent, manifold, and intimately involved with the essentials of their very existence. The poor are also less likely to enjoy ready access to legal counsel and more likely to suffer various forms of procedural discrimination.[1]

The original MFY Proposal did not anticipate the extent of the legal problems of the poor. Yet the proliferation of public social-welfare programs during the 1940's and 1950's had changed the entire relationship between law and the poor man. Administrators of city, state, and Federal agencies have enormous power to determine the dispensation of benefits of vital significance to the ghetto family, such as Aid to Dependent Children (ADC), Old Age Assistance (OAA), Aid to the Disabled (AD), and other welfare programs, public housing, unemployment compensation, etc. Although an individual's rights to receive these benefits and services are guaranteed under law, no rule of law governs the practices and procedures of the agencies which dispense them. To the contrary, a subtle denial of the legal rights of the poor often characterizes these practices.

[1] It has been pointed out that the lower middle class also cannot afford to pay for high-quality legal service. The rise of group legal services is in part a response to this problem.

Welfare and Housing Law

Welfare programs operate within the context of the strongly held national myth that America is the land of endless opportunity, that any man can succeed, given the virtue of thrift, self-reliance, good moral character, patience, hard work, etc. It has yet to be fully accepted that the burdens of the uneducated and unemployed must be borne by the society which has failed to provide education, jobs, or reasonable possibilities of obtaining them. Public agencies (and many private ones as well) persist in viewing the welfare client as a second- or third-class citizen because he is a public charge, as a fundamentally flawed individual incapable of assuming responsibility for his own life.

Holding fast to the idea of welfare benefits as gratuitously conferred privileges, welfare officials have considerable arbitrary power to confer or deny them. The privilege theory implicitly sanctions both wide administrative discretion and an almost total absence of procedural safeguards. There exist few means of enforcing the intent of legislation, no normative guidelines or standards for decision making, no procedure by which a client can discover the basis for a decision taken against him, and scant possibility of appeal. Where the possibility does exist, there is no general acquaintance with the procedures, and they are virtually never used. Many areas of welfare law are very poorly developed; no cases have been tried in them and hence no precedents set, because clients lack the knowledge and the means to challenge the system.

Originally established to mitigate the conditions of poverty and sustain its victims during a rehabilitation process, the relief programs as administered provide standards of living barely above subsistence levels, authorize extensive invasions of individual privacy, and encourage a situation of dependency. No program in the welfare state better illustrates the need for definition of rights, clarification of procedure, control of administrative discretion, and a means of enforcing rights and protecting recipients than does the welfare-relief program.

A second major source of legal difficulty for the poor in the welfare state is housing. The state, at least in New York, not only offers some public housing to aid the poor but attempts to control the quality and rents of private housing in ghetto areas by a wide series of legislative measures, including rent control, building-code regulations, penalties against landlords who fail to provide essential services, and various other methods. But these private-housing laws have been largely ineffective, in part because the housing available to the poor is scarce and is being reduced still further by highway construction and urban renewal. The courts have a functional legal bias in favor of the landlord, and in housing as in other spheres, the poor rarely know their legal rights or have the means to assert them. Because the interests of the low-income tenant have been inadequately supported, housing law is quite underdeveloped, and biases toward the owner are evident everywhere.

Such biases appear in the myriad of institutions and agencies with which a tenant who wishes to fight his landlord must deal and in the endless delays—often five or six months for a housing inspection—and red tape inhibiting his efforts to assert his rights. If the landlord can be found and brought to court, he will seldom receive more than a nominal fine, the courts being highly reluctant to prosecute an owner. The tenant, rarely possessing any knowledge of the law and seldom represented by a lawyer, finds himself faced with continual hearings, adjournments, postponements, etc., which the landlord's lawyer can easily afford while he often can not. If some action is finally taken on his original complaint, the tenant may find, the next time he wants his hot water turned on, that he again must confront the same tedious, difficult procedure.

In public housing the central fact underlying the problems of the poor is the law of supply and demand: Eighty-five thousand to 100,000 applications are received annually for eight thousand to ten thousand vacancies. This extreme pressure has led to questionable expediencies which reduce consideration of individual cases and increase a series of vague restrictive regulations. Tenancy for families already in projects can also be very insecure, for the privilege attitude is again applied. Public-housing authorities act as though space in a project is a favor extended to the tenant, and as though tenants do not have a right to fair eviction standards. Often eviction charges are so vague and general that no defense is possible. In the hearing no transcript, no lawyer, no confrontation and cross-examination of accusers, no investigation of evidence, and no standards of evidence are required. It becomes almost impossible for the tenant to refute the evidence and the overturning of an eviction is extremely rare.

Criminal Law

Crime is a poor man's problem. As compared to the nonpoor, he comes from conditions more conducive to it, he violates criminal law more often, and he is more likely to be caught and punished, the sentence often varying, again, with resources. The U.S. Attorney General's Committee, in its 1963 report "Poverty and the Administration of Federal Criminal Justice," stated:

> The infliction of gratuitous hardship on the impoverished has long been an ugly reality of the administration of justice. This cruelty is not only socially costly, it is also self-defeating; it promotes rather than deters crime, burdens rather than aids rehabilitation, provokes disrespect for law rather than encouraging social responsibility.

One of the most obvious disadvantages of the poor in criminal cases is the difficulty of finding bail money. The poor man jailed for lack of bail money is likely to lose his job and is unlikely to find a lawyer or witnesses. He has no chance in the interim before sentencing to prove his intention of reform—e.g., by getting into school or a job-training program—or otherwise to cast favorable light on his character. He emerges from confinement into the court poorly dressed, unshaven, and with prison pallor, none of which is likely to impress a judge favorably. Recent studies have shown that a defendant out on bail has a materially better chance of getting a lighter sentence or of not being convicted at all than a man who cannot raise his bail.

Consumer and Family Law

As regards consumer problems, the poor man has a larger proportion of his income tied up in debt payments and is more vulnerable because he has fewer savings to back up his debts. Moreover, he is particularly susceptible to compensatory spending—the effort to make up for the lack of status and prestige by the purchase of hard goods, the symbols of status. The poor are continually confronted with unfair and often unscrupulous practices. Merchants often take advantage of the consumer ignorance and the bad credit status of the poor, not only by simple fraud and overcharging, but by misrepresenting the price in vague contracts which do not include taxes, interest charges, or fees for installment buying. While merchants try to use persuasion and threats rather than legal sanctions, many families have experienced repossessions and garnishment of wages. Garnishment is particularly ugly, for most employers would rather fire an unskilled worker than become involved in legal procedures.

The family law of the poor is public law, administered largely through state and local agencies, more concerned with minimizing costs than with maximizing the rights and interests of the poor. In family-court dealings, there is a seemingly benign but actually insidious and quite dangerous paternalism—a way of prejudging the motives and the needs of the poor which implies that the poor are more apt to be stupid, in need of guidance and probably punishment, and less aware of themselves and their own self-interest than are those with more money. This condescending attitude can be seen in the position often taken on divorce by the poor, here stated by a California Legal Aid attorney: "People may say that poverty prevents the poor from having the same rights to get a divorce as a person with money, yet, we must remember, obtaining a divorce is not a right but a privilege. For most Legal Aid clients, a separation is just as useful and as practical as a divorce." [2]

[2] Jerome Carlin, Jan Howard, and Sheldon Messinger, "Civil Justice and the Poor," *Law and Society,* Vol. 1, (February, 1966), p. 59.

The Lawyers of the Poor

If their problems are recognized as legal in nature, the poor are then confronted with the unavailability of effective legal representation. Deprived of their just rights under law, the poor are further denied competent, aggressive legal counsel. It is an obvious fact that the well-to-do defendant has a much better chance of escaping imprisonment than has an indigent defendant, that the poor man's solution to the expense and legal complications of divorce is the common-law marriage, that in court a poor tenant is no match for a well-represented landlord, that the poor regard the law and lawyers as tools of the privileged, not as possible protectors of their interests. The then-Attorney General, Robert Kennedy, in an address at the University of Chicago on Law Day, May 1, 1964, said this about the failure of the legal profession to develop a rule of law for the poor:

> We have to begin asserting rights which the poor have always had in theory but which they have never been able to assert on their own behalf. Unasserted, unknown, unavailable rights are no rights at all. Lawyers must bear the responsibility for permitting the growth and continuance of two systems of law—one for the rich, one for the poor. Without a lawyer, of what use is the administrative review procedure set up under various welfare programs? Without a lawyer, of what use is the right to a partial refund for the payments made on a repossessed car? What is the price tag of equal justice under the law? Has simple justice a price which we as a profession must exact? [3]

In the same speech Mr. Kennedy commented, "To the poor man, 'legal' has become a synonym simply for technicalities and obstruction, not for that which is to be respected. The poor man looks upon the law as an enemy, not as a friend. For him the law is always taking something away." [4]

[3] Robert F. Kennedy, address on Law Day, May 1, 1964, University of Chicago Law School, as noted in Patricia M. Wald, "Law and Poverty: 1965." (Washington, D.C., National Conference on Law and Poverty, June 1965), working paper p. 2 note 5.

[4] *Ibid.*

In the past, if the poor realized the legal nature of their problem and sought to assert their rights, few possibilities for help were available, and all of them were very limited in effectiveness because of the economically inferior position of the client. One source of legal representation has long been the local political club, but the clubs on the Lower East Side are not, for the most part, involved with Puerto Ricans and Negroes. Their membership consists largely of earlier-arrived ethnic groups; they have yet to establish a working base among the latest immigrants, most of whom cannot or do not vote. A more common, but still not very popular, recourse is the private lawyer, privately retained—in this case, the marginal lawyer. He is usually a lawyer with an office in the neighborhood, but seldom does he live there or come from a similar social stratum or background; therefore he is likely to feel no particular identity with or responsibility to his clients. A study by the New York City bar has shown that these lawyers are the least competent, the least specialized in practice, and the least likely to conform to minimum standards of integrity. The resulting service for uneducated, low-status, high-turnover clients is remedial at best. The cases are mass-processed, for such a lawyer depends on a large volume of cases to sustain his practice. This means that he can spend very little time per case, which in turn usually leads, in criminal cases, to the waiving of the preliminary fact-finding hearing, since the lawyer cannot spare the time in court. This works to the extreme disadvantage of his client, for there is then less possibility of getting the charges reduced (which would involve a lower legal fee) or dismissed, and less chance of learning what evidence the prosecution has so that a proper defense can be prepared. It is not unusual for the marginal lawyer, after receiving his fee, to plead his client guilty, thereby obviating the need for extensive defense preparation in the case and eliminating the chance that the case might require more than the minimal expenditure of time in court. These practices justify the common lower-class fears of being sold out by a lawyer.

The most publicized source of legal help for the poor is the Legal Aid Society. Legal Aid as an organization is handicapped by the manner in which it is organized and financed, and by its conception of its task. Its main limitation is its restrictive policy in accepting cases, both in terms of eligibility and in the substance of the cases themselves. In some areas, for example, clients who earn more than $1,500 a year are ineligible for service. Legal Aid is an old, well-organized, and established agency, often directed by prominent community leaders, with most of the routine and bureaucratization that this fact implies. Because of self-limitations, Legal Aid does no proselytizing on its own behalf. Its offices are usually in the center of a city and therefore inaccessible to most of the poor population, whose worlds are defined by their neighborhoods. The location of the offices, combined with the client's general fears about the law and officials and bureaucracies, may put a visit to Legal Aid out of their realm of possibilities. To compound the problem further, these remote offices do not advertise, and their printed publicity is confined to a listing in the phone book.

Legal Aid agencies have failed to educate the poor about their rights in cases of civil law. Because they lack funds and time, they operate for the most part on a one-shot basis, with no investigations of or long-term plans for the prevention of the problems that tenants, consumers, and applicants for government benefits bring to them. As a result of all these limitations, most Legal Aid agencies have failed to grow. A Detroit study has shown that only 1.3 percent of the poor have ever had contact with Legal Aid. Nine major cities (those with 100,000+ population) are without Legal Aid societies at all, and twenty-four of the others have societies that do not meet the legal minimum requirements of the American Bar Association and the National Legal Aid and Defenders Association.

The Legal Aid Society puts strict limitations on the type of cases it will accept. Until recently, no divorce cases were taken in New York City. Now only a few are handled, and these must meet strict standards of "social necessity." One apparent reason for this restriction is the desire to minimize the cost of public aid, as shown in two statements by Legal Aid attorneys:

Our experience is that indigents already have a large family supported by the community, and to permit them a free divorce allows the man particularly to remarry, frequently a much younger woman, and to procreate a fresh batch of public charges.

It has been learned through experience that nearly all divorce cases involving indigents, where the husband is not incarcerated for some reason or other, are merely a device to entitle the wife and children to go on public-assistance rolls.

In these statements the individual is viewed as a welfare client receiving privileges, rather than as a citizen capable of knowing his own best interests while obtaining his just rights under law.

From the point of view of the poor, Legal Aid's effectiveness is hampered by its grossly inadequate resources for the large job it is supposed to undertake, its vulnerability to the demands and pressures of local bar associations and businessmen, and its adoption of social-welfare attitudes toward clients and their goals.

As regards criminal cases, New York's Legal Aid Society has been providing comprehensive free legal counsel to indigents in both state and Federal courts for some twenty years. It was given impetus to enlarge in 1962, when the newly created Family Court required counsel for all juvenile delinquents, and again in 1963, upon the Supreme Court's *Gideon v. Wainwright* decision, requiring counsel for indigents in all felony cases. Today New York's Legal Aid Society's criminal division is probably the best in the country; yet certain problems remain.

The society offers the indigent defendant counsel at each step in the judicial process, but this means a different lawyer at each step: One lawyer will represent the defendant at his arraignment, a second at his trial, etc. The system is constructed this way for reasons of economic and administrative efficiency; each lawyer becomes highly specialized in the procedure of his court, and thus able to deal with each case efficiently and quickly; trial mistakes are reduced to a minimum; rapid disposal of a case is more likely. The trouble with this approach is that the defendant may have to deal with four or more attorneys as his case progresses through the court system. The large volume of cases each attorney must handle, owing to the preponderance of low-income people in criminal cases, means hasty and fragmented assistance to each client. The attorney who has to dispose of forty cases a day can afford only ten or fifteen minutes per case, considering that he has to scan previous records, make reports, etc., and this leaves him little time to discuss the case with the defendant or to explain the situation to him.[5]

For the defendant, confronted with a serious crisis in his life, the rushed treatment by his lawyer, the lack of an opportunity to tell his side of the story, and the succession of unfamiliar lawyers can be terrifying. When an attorney hastily interviews his client in a noisy, confusing detention pen, the defendant cannot communicate clearly or tell his story in full detail; he concludes that the lawyer is either disinterested or incompetent, which confirms his suspicions about the whole judicial process. The time constraint prevents the attorney not only from hearing out his client, but also from explaining the judicial process to him or playing any sort of supportive role. The problem of fragmentation means that the attorney must sometimes sacrifice defense remedies [6] since he cannot leave the courtroom for fear that a case of his might be called; therefore he may have no contact with a case before he is to present it in court. He will then have to rely on records made by his predecessors and must be sure his own records are accurate for his successors. One of the most serious consequences of the huge case load of the Legal Aid Society and the serially fragmented nature of its legal assistance is the impossibility of providing indigents with the personal treatment, comprehensive in-depth legal counsel, and carefully prepared defense and follow-up help required to make the public

[5] In many areas other than New York there is little time for pretrial investigation or for locating witnesses, and a shorthand method for conducting a defense develops, which means getting only the most basic information and devising a strategy for negotiating a settlement with the prosecution. New York Legal Aid maintains a staff of former detectives to do pretrial investigative work.

[6] He cannot, for example, leave the court to obtain a writ of habeas corpus.

goal of equal justice under the law a reality in the criminal courts.[7]

The MFY Legal Unit

The original proposal on which MFY was based, despite its broad range of activities and sophisticated theoretical perspective, did not anticipate either the legal ramifications of its programs or the relevance of the legal profession to MFY's aims, and therefore made no provision for the inclusion of a legal unit. The need to involve the legal profession became apparent after a few months. The Legal Services Unit is, in effect, a product of lessons learned early in Mobilization's experience on the Lower East Side.

In early 1963 it was decided to have the legal problems confronting both MFY programs and their clients investigated by the Vera Foundation, a Manhattan philanthropic institution well-known for its Bail Reform Project and other legal-reform interests. At MFY's request, the foundation drew up a plan for a legal unit with the following three functions: (1) direct service to and referral of clients; (2) legal orientation for MFY staff, clients, and community leaders; (3) use of law as an instrument of social change.

The Legal Unit was to consist of a director, one or two assistant attorneys, and a pool of volunteer lawyers, who would handle cases particularly pertinent to MFY's interests or research aims. Most of the cases were to be referred to the Legal Aid Society or the Consumer Fraud Bureau.

An important function of the Legal Unit was to make legal processes and their implications comprehensible to the MFY staff and clients, both by drawing up materials regarding basic rights and obligations in housing, welfare, workman's compensation, and installment-buying and by sponsoring legal-orientation clinics run

[7] Steps are being taken to meet some of these problems. Additional staff has made it possible for one lawyer to handle a juvenile's case throughout the judicial process, and the society appears to be interested in establishing neighborhood offices which, with adequate resources, could facilitate a more comprehensive and personal treatment of indigent defendants. The problems outlined above reflect less upon the Legal Aid Society, which does remarkably well given its financial and administrative resources, than upon a well-endowed society which permits the continuance of a situation which leads to such conditions.

by volunteer lawyers to educate the community in its legal rights and to elicit cases.

Although MFY accepted the report of the Vera Foundation for administrative reasons, it declined the foundation's offer to establish a program and set out to construct one of its own. The MFY plan was almost identical to the Vera proposal, incorporating the major principles, suggested organizational format, and supporting arguments, except that MFY decided to use the Columbia Law School faculty and student body in a supervisory and advisory capacity. A starting grant was obtained from the Department of Health, Education and Welfare in November 1963.

A major issue was getting authorization to offer free legal services to the poor. The New York Penal Law then prohibited corporations from practicing law. Exceptions were made for organizations with benevolent or charitable purposes, provided that they received authorization from the Appellate Division of the Supreme Court of New York. Such authorization had previously been given only to Legal Aid and the city bar association. Approval of MFY's application by the New York courts was stalled by the issue of competition with Legal Aid and was not granted until the bar association gave its approval with the specification that the MFY Legal Unit was to be a temporary activity, of an experimental nature, and that it would not duplicate work done by Legal Aid.

As regards the three major functions of the unit outlined in the Vera proposal—direct service and referral, legal orientation of MFY clients and staff, and use of law as an instrument of social change—the director of the Legal Unit concluded that the first two were of minimal importance as compared to the foremost function of the unit: the use of the law as an instrument for social change.

With its general orientation toward social change, MFY assumed that the legal test case was to be the primary vehicle for creating new law as well as establishing the rule of law in the administrative processes of welfare programs. The most important legal needs of the poor were seen as those which concerned their relations with government-sponsored welfare programs. These were areas of the law largely unserved by the legal profession, involving issues generally defined in a way that precluded legal intervention. In a

January 1964 memorandum, "Poverty, Law, and Social Welfare," Edward Sparer, the director of the program, enunciated the basic policy of the Legal Services Unit.[8] The memorandum states a philosophical justification for representing poor clients of government agencies, documents the poor client's need for legal representation in matters of welfare, housing, and civil and criminal law, and proposes several programs and strategies for the unit. Accepting the notion that welfare benefits are rights, Sparer argues for the need to develop a rule of law in the administration of welfare programs. He asserts that access to skilled legal help, independent of control by the government agency involved, is a basic requirement of the "effective remedy, fair procedure, and reasoned decision" to which claimants are entitled. A series of studies is suggested which would focus initially on applications of New York's Welfare Abuse Law, the disuse of federally guaranteed fair-hearing procedures in welfare disputes, and violations of individuals' right to privacy by early morning raids and other unreasonable investigatory practices by the Department of Welfare. In each situation, litigation is assumed where appropriate.

In the housing area, the memorandum outlines the ineffectiveness of legislation designed to promote decent housing conditions for the poor—receivership, rent reduction, code enforcement, etc.— and argues that a major part of the problem is the lack of lawyers to insist on enforcement of the present housing legislation.

In cases involving unemployment insurance, where an adequate system of appeals existed, the unit was to provide counsel, previously unavailable at appeals hearings, and to explore the relevance of previously unused portions of the state unemployment law.

The memo describes three functions for the unit in the promotion of equal justice under criminal law. The first involves representation of indigent defendants at the police station house, where the defendant is most likely to do himself damage through inadvertent admissions or coerced statements. Accordingly, the unit would make counsel available to youths of the MFY area "upon arrest and booking at the police station." A second function involved the

[8] Edward Sparer, "Poverty, Law, and Social Welfare" (mimeographed, New York, Mobilization For Youth, January, 1964).

need for "developing a set of norms, as well as safeguards, for the determination of the dispositional issues in the postconviction stages of criminal proceedings." The unit would develop a defense attorney's role for representation of youth in probation and related postconviction matters. The third function outlined in the criminal-law field was a preventive one. It was suggested that a properly trained attorney, in conjunction with a gang worker, could interact with "gang members and other youths in such a way as to increase their respect for the prohibitions of the law and to encourage their utilization of the constructive work and other opportunities made available to them by such social agencies as MFY."

In consumer law, the memo proposed that the Legal Unit handle those cases which could be settled without extensive litigation and refer the more difficult cases to Legal Aid. Accompanying the representation, it was proposed that the unit undertake a program of consumer education for selected MFY staff and local residents.

The memorandum concludes by setting forth a referral policy for civil cases which are normally handled by the Legal Aid Society. According to this statement, the Legal Unit would undertake an educational program for MFY and local-agency social workers and community leaders, to equip them to refer civil cases to the director of the unit. The director would then determine whether the case should be handled within the unit. "All traditional civil-law problems which cannot be settled by immediate negotiation will be referred to the Legal Aid Society."

In January 1964, "Poverty, Law and Society" was approved as MFY's policy statement. The papers which follow in this section examine both the results achieved by the Legal Unit and the changes in original policy which experience dictated.[9]

[9] Yearly budgets for the division were as follows: 1963–64, $35,120.00; 1964–65, $65,311.00; 1965–66, $118,090.00; 1966–67, $304,633.00. The figures do not include indirect costs for fiscal services, executive offices, public information, central services, personnel department, and occupancy costs. Indirect costs averaged an additional 25 percent a year. The President's Committee on Juvenile Delinquency and the Office of Economic Opportunity were the major funding sources.

2

The Effect of Legal Counsel on Criminal Cases

Michael Appleby

Crime and poverty bear a close relationship. The poor supply a disproportionate share of this country's criminal defendants, and the slums traditionally experience the highest crime rates. Moreover, the poor suffer disproportionately at the hands of the law. They are the prime targets of clean-up campaigns and dragnet investigative arrests. They are less cognizant of their legal rights and consequently more likely to make confessions or admissions damaging to their interests. Conviction follows as a matter of course.

While the poor defendant must be assigned counsel in a felony case, the right to counsel in misdemeanor cases has not been established on a national basis. A poor defendant's first contact with a lawyer is usually at his arraignment, but a lawyer may be most valuable to him at prearraignment proceedings. Further, it has been shown that the bail system discriminates in favor of the more affluent. One observer describes the operation of the system as follows:

> . . . [the defendant] faces the problem of raising bail money or
> spending months in jail awaiting grand jury indictment or trial. . . .
> If it [the money] cannot be raised and the breadwinner goes to jail
> to await trial, his family may be thrown onto relief, evicted from
> public housing, or broken up. In jail the accused cannot locate or
> persuade defense witnesses to appear. Assigned counsel, rarely com-

pensated for out-of-pocket expenses or given investigative help, must prepare the defense unaided. At sentencing, the poor defendant who has been in jail since his arrest has a reduced chance of establishing his rehabilitative potential for probation as a job holder, stable family man, and integrated member of the community. Often he is imprisoned solely because he cannot pay a fine.

Despite bail-reform programs and recent court decisions which afford the poor additional legal protections, the poor defendant still receives far from equal treatment at the hands of the law.

At the outset, Mobilization's criminal representation was intended to complement the activities of other organizations providing legal services to the poor rather than to duplicate existing programs. An analysis was undertaken to identify those areas in which MFY's small legal staff could make the maximal contribution to legal service for indigent defendants. The program which emerged included the following innovations:

1. The provision of legal counsel to defendants at the police station house;
2. The extension of the attorney's role to include post-conviction probation proceedings and related matters;
3. Efforts in conjunction with local detached gang workers to encourage youthful defendants to utilize work programs and other opportunities made available by social agencies, churches, etc.

In addition, the program included activities supplemental to the work of the Legal Aid Society. Thus the Legal Unit was to act as a feeder system, referring routine criminal cases to Legal Aid. Cases requiring extensive investigation or preparation were to be handled within the unit. The unit was also to assist in the preparation of a defense for Lower East Side residents charged with a crime. Unit attorneys were to gather defense witnesses and investigate as needed.

Once the Legal Unit was in operation, it met conditions somewhat different from those originally expected and began to re-

evaluate its role, particularly regarding referral to Legal Aid and
the scope of the unit's orientation. Three major goals evolved with
regard to criminal law: (1) the provision of comprehensive, high-
quality legal representation on a neighborhood basis; (2) breaking the cycle of recidivism among defendants; (3) the use of the
law as an instrument of social change.

Each of these goals influences the kind of cases accepted, the
treatment of clients, and the nature of the services offered.

A Comprehensive Service

In order to make high-quality legal representation readily ac-
cessible to the neighborhood, law offices have been established in
decentralized locations. The offices themselves remain open through
early evening, but the unit maintains a twenty-four-hour emergency
service for arrested individuals and their families, and a mobile
office-unit circulates through the neighborhood to increase the
accessibility of unit services.

Between January 1965 and May 1967, the Legal Unit handled
a total of 1,252 criminal cases, averaging seventy-three cases a
month. The two most popular categories are cases involving drug
charges and disorderly-conduct complaints. The drug cases include
alleged possession of marijuana, heroin, or amphetamines, possession of "works"—a needle and a cooker for heroin or amphetamines—and drug sales. Marijuana and heroin are the drugs most
commonly encountered. Recently, however, there have been several
cases involving the possession or sale of LSD and amphetamines.
Unit attorneys prefer not to accept drug-sales cases because they
are usually difficult to defend successfully, and the resources of the
unit can contribute little to the outcome.

Disorderly-conduct charges typically include assault, fighting,
resisting arrest, or creating a commotion. They are frequently the
result of friction between the police and the community, particularly Negro and Puerto Rican youths. Groups of young Puerto
Ricans or Negroes are often broken up or told to move on;
minority-group members who drive cars are often stopped and

questioned. Such practices naturally create resentment and resistance, which in turn results in arrests for disorderly conduct.

The remainder of the case load consists of occasional burglary or robbery complaints and miscellaneous charges. Gang fighting is virtually nonexistent.

The number of cases unit attorneys can accept at any given time is limited by the limited resources of the Legal Unit. If the volume of cases which remain outstanding were allowed to become very large, the unit would face the same problems as Legal Aid. At present, most of the unit's criminal case load is handled by two full-time and one part-time lawyer. Several unit attorneys who specialize in other legal areas accept a small number of criminal cases each month. Although each of these lawyers is free to establish his own criteria for accepting a case (within the income requirements laid down by the Office of Economic Opportunity), a consistent set of standards has been formulated according to which unit attorneys accept a case or refer it to Legal Aid. Assistance is normally provided by the Legal Unit in cases in which any of the following conditions is present:

1. The defendant is a first offender (adult or youth). The defendant's initial experience with the law is thought to be of crucial importance. Personal treatment, guidance, and follow-up are regarded as essential if the first encounter is to be a constructive experience.

2. The defendant is involved in a MFY program, has had experience with MFY activities, or can be enrolled in such a program.

3. The defendant's criminal behavior is related to psychological, social, or economic problems which are amenable to other forms of intervention—social work, etc.

4. The case requires the kind of pretrial investigation, defense preparation, and continuing personal attention that Legal Aid cannot provide effectively. Such cases are those in which the personal treatment and comprehensive assistance offered by the unit might make a difference in the judicial outcome.

5. Unorthodox cases which are not accepted by the Legal Aid Society. Such cases often raise questions of a controversial moral or political nature.

6. Cases which involve police brutality, harassment, or questions of improper search and seizure (commonly associated with drug cases).

The potential impact of a case on the unit's relationship with the community is also taken into account, when the defendant is well-known and liked in the neighborhood. The services provided to a criminal defendant are as comprehensive as possible, and the processes involved are explained carefully.

The assigned attorney handles the defendant's case from the initial interview through trial and posttrial proceedings. Thus he is in a position to establish a personal relationship with the defendant. He is available to the client, time permitting, whenever the client wants to see him, and he tries to give the client detailed consideration. One observer describes the lawyer's activities in this way:

> The defendant and witnesses are spoken to at length, often more than once. Their stories and backgrounds are carefully considered, and a thoughtful decision is reached on who should and should not testify. Where necessary, character witnesses are prepared (usually persons in charge of some MFY program). The scene of the alleged incident will be visited and photographed when needed. A decision to advise a client to plead guilty will be based on a thorough knowledge of the case and a careful evaluation of the possibility of securing an acquittal after trial.

The time spent with a defendant is of critical importance to the unit's second goal—breaking the chain of recidivism. The neighborhood location of the unit facilitates contact and makes the posttrial follow-up of a client easier for the unit attorney.

In addition to in-depth interviews of the defendant by an attorney, the unit provides resources for the pretrial investigation of a case which otherwise would not be possible. Moreover, it is possible for the unit to conduct the pretrial investigation soon after the incident in question and thereby reduce the loss of witnesses and evidence to a minimum. Social workers and Vista volunteers attached to the unit are available to investigate the defendant's family, work, or school situation, locate and interview witnesses, and gather field material of use in the preparation of a legal defense. As noted previously, such pretrial investigation is often crucial to successful defense against a criminal charge. Nonlegal personnel attached to the unit also file court papers, maintain contact with a defendant or his family, etc.

Another important factor which contributes to the overall quality of representation is the unit's relationship to other MFY programs. The Legal Unit has been able to make use of Mobilization's work and training programs, to the great advantage of its clients. In addition, MFY social workers, consulting psychiatrists, youth counselors, etc., are invaluable aids in the investigation, analysis, and preparation of a defense, its presentation in court, and follow-up. The availability of legal, social, and psychiatric resources enables the unit to deal with a client's problem on a variety of levels, which helps to offset the disadvantageous position of the indigent defendant in the judicial process.

Breaking the Chain of Recidivism

The assumption behind the unit's approach to recidivism is that criminal acts have social, economic, and psychological origins and will recur unless these basic causes are removed. The environmental factors which give rise to criminal behavior must be attacked if the judicial process is to have a correctional effect. Thus, for a youthful defendant, the assistance given by social workers attached to the unit would extend beyond his legal defense and might include helping his family with the Welfare Department, finding him a job, enrolling him in a training program, and obtaining psychiatric help. It would also include follow-up assistance if he were convicted. In numerous instances a young defendant in a criminal case has returned to the unit for help with his family's welfare and housing problems. Unit staff try to probe beyond the presenting problem to ascertain whether the client faces other problems amenable to legal intervention. In the unit's view, breaking the chain of recidivism requires both removal of the environmental pressures which encourage the recurrence of criminal behavior and creation of new opportunities and behavior patterns.

Closely related to the guidance the unit provides for a defendant are its efforts to educate the larger community about the law. Unit attorneys hold seminars with local groups and provide young people with wallet cards informing them of their right to remain silent upon arrest and their right to legal counsel, and listing where legal assistance might be obtained. Although few defendants remember the card and its uses in time of crisis, friends or relatives often do remember and contact the unit.

Legal Unit attorneys try to make an encounter with the law a learning experience for the defendant. The absence of case-load pressures allows the MFY lawyer time to hear the defendant's story in full. Unit lawyers take pains to explain the meaning of each step of the judicial process to the defendant, what his options are, and, of course, what he can expect next. Their purpose is to combat the defendant's feeling—often justified—that he is being sold out or that the system is out to get him. This is regarded as especially important for a youthful offender in his first contact with the law, and also for adult first offenders terrified of the possible consequences of their scrape with the law.

Recent studies have shown that a defendant who is out on bail has a materially better chance of receiving a light sentence or not being convicted; therefore, one of the main goals of the Legal Unit is to get clients freed on low bail. Unit lawyers repeatedly petition the court to reduce the bail to an amount the defendant can afford. The results of these efforts have been remarkable. For example, the unit director reports that of seventy-five defendants represented in the winter of 1967, all but one were released on bail. Without the unit's pressure on behalf of low bail, most of the defendants would be forced to stay in jail until their case came to trial.

The attempt to get unit clients out of jail is functionally related to a second important aspect of unit strategy. Once defendants are freed on bail, unit attorneys try to place them in a constructive environment, with the twofold intent of establishing a basis for winning probation and reducing their contact with the environment which produced or encouraged the original criminal behavior. This has been found to be an effective method of keeping young defendants out of jail, aiding them on probation, and involving in school, job, or community programs youths who otherwise would not participate.

The consistent experience of the unit has been that judges are most lenient when, as one observer puts it . . .

> . . . the lawyer can tell the court that the defendant is now working or is in a job-training program, that his employer speaks highly of him, that the defendant has voluntarily gone for psychiatric help, or that he is enrolled in the MFY college-preparatory course.

The unit has frequenty found that defendants who have such supportive reports often receive sympathetic treatment from the courts while less fortunate defendants are dealt with more harshly. Lighter sentences and a greater incidence of probation are the result of the unit's close relationship with programs of MFY and other community institutions.

Unit attorneys continue to work with a client upon his return to the community on parole or after serving a prison sentence, to help him avoid further involvement with the law. One important dimension of follow-up care concerns the client's relationship to his parole officer. The unit sees to it that a client knows his rights and obligations, and unit lawyers often intercede in instances of parole officer–client conflict. The advocacy of a parolee's interest is regarded as an important source of support in the tenuous process of reestablishing his life in the community.

In sum, the legal strategy of the unit in breaking the chain of recidivism consists of the following elements:

1. The total-law approach, aimed at removing the environmental factors which contribute to criminal behavior.

2. Education of the community to its rights and obligations with regard to criminal law.

3. Legal representation of defendants in criminal cases, including

    (a) representation on an individual basis

    (b) pretrial investigation

    (c) efforts to minimize time spent in jail awaiting trial, by persuading court to reduce bail

    (d) emphasis upon making the experience a learning one for the defendant

    (e) utilization of community, school, social-agency, and employment resources for the integration of a defendant into community life

    (f) posttrial follow-up and assistance.

The Law as an Instrument of Social Change [1]

The Legal Unit's orientation toward social change, so evident in its work in welfare, housing, and other areas, was also manifested in its practice of criminal law. However, the unit's impact upon the content of the criminal law and the administration of justice in criminal cases has been negligible, for three major reasons: the established character of the criminal-court system and its resistance to change; the lack of sufficient cases which raise appeal issues; and the particular demands upon the attorney-client relationship in criminal cases.

Criminal law appears to be less susceptible to dramatic change than other areas of law which affect the poor, in part because concepts of criminal law and procedures of criminal justice are well defined in Anglo-Saxon judicial tradition. Attitudes and practices of the lower criminal courts are strongly entrenched, and the rate of change is slow. Further, the source of change in criminal law is not located at the state level, where the majority of cases are

[1] For an informed appraisal of MFY's overall achievement as a change agent by means of the Legal Unit's efforts, see the chapter by Harold Rothwax, current director of the Legal Unit, "The Law as an Instrument of Social Change" in this volume.

adjudicated. Rather, the stimulus for change has come from the United States Supreme Court and the Federal court system. Moreover, as a general rule, the courts are reluctant to sit in judgment of the legislature. They prefer to see that the law is properly applied rather than themselves decide constitutional issues.

The narrow base upon which appeals can be made is another major factor hampering attempts to alter the criminal court system. Few cases handled by the unit raise issues which can be appealed; therefore, the unit lacks the requisite volume of cases to make effective challenges. The most important cases in the criminal area have involved issues of procedure rather than substance.

Another problem is the particular vulnerability of the defendant in criminal cases, and the responsibility of an attorney to represent his client as effectively as possible. A central tenet of the legal profession holds that the interest of the client is to have priority over all other considerations, that the lawyer is to do nothing which in any way weakens the client's best interest. In criminal cases, the issues frequently have extremely serious consequences for the defendant; his job, liberty, and future may depend on the outcome. Winning a favorable decision is often much more crucial for a defendant in a criminal case than for a welfare recipient, a tenant, or a litigant in a consumer-fraud case. The implications of this fact for successful appeal are obvious. In cases which present good issues for appeal, the prosecution will usually offer to reduce the charges against the defendant in exchange for a plea of guilty. The attorney is faced with the choice of pressing the case and running the risk of losing, or accepting the certainty of a light or suspended sentence for his client. If the reduction is significant and the original charges involve a lengthy incarceration, it is clearly in the interest of the defendant to accept the offer. In this event the possibility of an appeal must be foregone.

In addition, the attorney often cannot be sure that the defendant has been entirely candid; he may therefore fear that the defense will be quickly defeated in court if unexpected evidence is introduced. The attorney must take such considerations into account in deciding whether to advise his client to plead guilty in exchange for a lighter sentence. In this sense the district attorney has a very real advantage in his ability to buy out cases which might involve serious challenges to court procedures or to some aspect of criminal law.

In sum, the unit attorneys must work in an environment resistant to change, with a limited number of cases subject to appeal, and with defendants whose willingness to pursue an appeal is easily compromised. Under such conditions, it is not surprising that little change has resulted from the unit's practice of criminal law.

The unit's important attempts to effect change have thus far involved procedural issues. Two practices have been challenged: the detention of a material witness by the prosecution as a means of extracting desired testimony, and the denial of a preliminary hearing. Each case illustrates certain problems attendant to the goal of social change.[2]

Material Witness

New York law allows the district attorney to hold in lieu of bail a witness considered to be "material and necessary" to the state's case. Ironically, it is possible to have a defendant free on bail and a witness still in jail. In practice this provision of the law is used to extract the desired information from a reluctant witness. The possibility of staying in jail until the trial is held, which may be a year later, encourages most witnesses to agree to testify.

Ronaldo M., for example, was arrested in consequence of an unsubstantiated rumor that he had not only been present at the fatal shooting of a store owner but had also provided the defendant with the murder weapon. There were no witnesses to Ronaldo's presence at the crime. He was originally arrested for possession of a gun, but the charges were dismissed for lack of substantive evi-

[2] The U. S. Supreme Court refused to hear a case originated in the Legal Unit which claimed that a client's inability to raise bail and therefore his subsequent detention was a denial of equal protection and due process. The Legal Unit has also petitioned the Supreme Court to hear a case in which it is argued that the possession of marijuana for one's own use is not, constitutionally, a crime.

dence. Upon his release, Ronaldo was rearraigned as a material witness on the ground that his testimony was necessary to the prosecution of the homicide. The unit attorney asked for a hearing, but his request was denied. A habeas corpus was filed, and the State Supreme Court judge requested the original judge to allow a hearing. In that court, bail was set at $10,000, and a motion to dismiss the petition on the basis of hearsay was rejected. After three weeks had passed, another hearing was held as required by law, and the material-witness allegation was dismissed for lack of evidence. A challenge to the practice of holding material witnesses was no longer possible once the charges had been dropped.

Ronaldo M.'s case is a good example of how a good appeal may be lost when a case is won. It is also a prime example of the value of legal counsel. The prosecutor of this case admitted privately that he did not need Ronaldo and probably would not call him, inasmuch as more reliable witnesses were available.

The Preliminary Hearing

The other important challenge undertaken by the unit relates to the practice, evident in the Ronaldo M. case, of denying preliminary hearings to the defense. Such hearings give the defense attorney an opportunity to learn the evidence against his client and to have the charges reduced or dismissed. District attorneys therefore attempt to persuade the court against preliminary hearings. In cases involving serious charges, the state generally requests a series of adjournments, in the meantime presenting the case before the grand jury. When the defendants in one such case were denied a preliminary hearing, the unit attorney brought an order to compel the state to grant a preliminary hearing, as required by law. The opportunity to obtain a ruling which might have provided general relief was lost when the judge then offered to reduce the charge from a felony to a misdemeanor if the attorney would forego the hearing. The offer was clearly to the defendant's interest and was accepted. Similar instances occur repeatedly and make it difficult to have any impact on the administration of criminal justice.

Although both of the cases reviewed above were settled to the advantage of the defendants, the abuses they illustrate continue.

Conclusions

Some people scoff at the idea of Mobilization's providing a lawyer for a person accused of stealing MFY property. Yet a society founded on law must make sure that the law applies equally to rich and poor. The Legal Unit in its criminal cases demonstrated the extent to which this ideal has been violated. A man is truly an outcast when he has no hope of becoming part of society. When laws are arbitrarily interpreted and consistently abused, then they further diminish feelings of hope and encourage the development of a society of criminals.

The ability of the Legal Unit to utilize the services of the other MFY divisions, education, work, and family services not only worked to the considerable advantage of defendants, but also illustrated the need for such arrangements with lawyers who practice in the criminal courts. Private social agencies would do well to develop working relationships with Legal Aid societies as well as with individual lawyers who specialize in criminal law.

3

Family Law and the Poor

Michael Appleby and Henry Heifetz

Of all social institutions, the family is perhaps the most seriously affected by poverty. It is on the family that overcrowded housing, uncertain, irregular, and poorly paid employment, and the economic and personal limitations imposed by indigency have their greatest impact. Although the Legal Services Unit did not explicitly undertake to help individual families in the Lower East Side, a significant portion of its case load is composed of troubled families which have become involved with the law.

There are two major areas to the unit's activities in domestic-relations law: (a) divorce and separation cases, and (b) cases which involve serious family crises, such as juvenile delinquency, predelinquent behavior problems, child-neglect petitions, and child custody.

Cases involving family-related or domestic-relations issues accounted for 12 to 16 percent of the monthly case load. Divorce or separation actions constituted 45 percent of these. Some 42 percent of the cases involved family members who faced some form of legal proceedings in Family Court. Child-custody and adoption actions accounted for another 10 percent of the domestic-relations cases.

Divorce and Separation Cases

New York divorce law until recently has been a good example of de facto bias in the law governing marital relations. Until the revision of the laws effective September 1967, the only ground for divorce was adultery. While the law applied equally to all New York residents regardless of income, its effect was unequal, inasmuch as some out-of-state decrees were recognized. Consequently, those with the financial resources to travel were able to obtain divorces which were not available to the poor. One observer describes the effect of out-of-state divorce in the following way:

> Since a migratory divorce is usually more expensive than one secured locally, this pattern of evasion is not equally open to all New Yorkers. If state laws are easily avoided by financially independent residents, they can be avoided by others only at some sacrifice, and avoided not at all by those with low incomes. In this sense, the laws impinge differentially on the population. . . .[1]

There are, of course, other options open to the poor. These include annulment, formal separation, termination of the marriage if one of the members had been absent over five years and was presumed dead, desertion, and fraudulent legal action. While one observer suggests that the discriminatory effect of New York divorce laws upon the poor contributed to a more permissive attitude of the bench toward indigents seeking a divorce,[2] the poor man's divorce was generally a legal separation arranged with the help of the Legal Aid Society, or simple desertion.[3] Frequently new con-

---

[1] Jerome Carlin, Jan Howard, and Sheldon Messinger, "Civil Justice and the Poor," *Law and Society*, Vol. 1, (February 1966), p. 22.

[2] See, R. Wells, "New York: The Poor Man's Reno," *Cornell Law Quarterly*, Vol. 35, (1950), pp. 303–26. Wells observes: "It is, perhaps, a judicial awareness of the ease with which quick solutions to marital complexities are available to those able to pay for them and a judicial sense of fairness that has caused our judges to turn New York into a poor man's Reno for all with sufficiently elastic consciences" (p. 315).

[3] For a detailed analysis of the New York Family Court Act of 1962, see Nanette Dembitz, "Ferment and Experiment in New York: Juvenile Cases in New York Family Court," *Cornell Law Quarterly*, Vol. 48 (1963), pp. 499–523.

sensual unions were formed after the break in the marital relationship.

The pattern of informal accommodation or formal separation, with the assumption of new marital relations and responsibilities after the first marriage, created large numbers of families whose marital relationships required a number of adjustments before they could be legally recognized. In most instances, divorces had to be obtained and remarriages arranged before the tie could be legalized and children legitimized. Much of the unit's work with divorce and separation has come out of the backlog of legally unresolved marital relationships created by a narrow, discriminatory divorce law.

The revision of New York divorce legislation has had the effect of releasing the pent-up demand for divorces. In addition to liberalizing the grounds for divorce, the new legislation, although requiring a two-year separation, has essentially made divorce a mere formality. Under the new law, the parties are to work out a separation agreement which details the terms of support, child custody, and visiting rights. If, after a two-year period of separation, it can be shown that the terms of the agreement have been fulfilled, a divorce is a simple formality and easily obtained.

Since the law has gone into effect, the unit has had a sizable increase in the number of clients seeking divorces or legal separations. A unit attorney who specializes in Family Court cases has found that many individuals, who had to settle for separation, the poor man's divorce, and have in the meantime set up new households, now want to get a divorce, remarry, and have their children legitimized. In such cases, the function of the Legal Unit is simply to provide advice on the separation agreement and representation in the court proceedings.

The unit is one of a number of organizations providing this service. For example, the Legal Aid Society has established a special unit to handle such cases. Compared to the huge numbers of cases handled by Legal Aid and similar agencies, the unit's monthly total of about twenty divorce or separation cases may seem insignificant.[4] Nevertheless, assistance with divorces is a necessary function, as some clients are intimidated by a trip out of the neighborhood to another, more imposing, agency.

The Family Court System of New York

Almost all of the unit's family-related cases involve Family Court proceedings. New York Family Court deals with five categories of problems: (1) juvenile delinquency—behavior which, if the offender were an adult, would lead to prosecution under a criminal statute; (2) predelinquent behavior problems, which involve minor offenses, truancy, and school discipline; (3) child-neglect petitions brought against parents who abuse their children or fail to provide adequately for them; (4) child-custody and adoption cases; and (5) parent problems and issues of family non-support.

Under a reorganization of the Family Court system in 1962, juvenile defendants were provided with counsel, and the rights of young defendants were clarified. According to the principles underlying the revision of the court, the judicial process is to be guided by the intent to meet the program or therapeutic needs of juvenile defendants. The court sessions as a consequence are less formal, the requirements of testimony and evidence are more relaxed, and the confrontation between prosecution and defense is less openly adversarial than in adult criminal-court proceedings.[5] In theory, the relaxation of formal requirements of process allows the court to deal more flexibly with young defendants and to arrive at solutions which are more responsive to their needs. The orientation of the court is to be therapeutic and ameliorative rather than punitive.

However, the effectiveness of this orientation in practice depends

[4] The Legal Unit is, however, concerning itself with the important problem of additional costs involved in getting a divorce besides legal fees—costs of publishing notices in newspapers. Legal Aid Society will not file divorce proceedings unless the client can pay these costs, which can amount to $300. The Legal Unit has several actions pending in which they argue the right of a client to a divorce even if he cannot afford the related fees.

[5] These conditions are under review in cases yet to be decided by the U. S. Supreme Court.

not only upon the attitudes of the judges but also upon the adequacy of the parole system, the availability of supportive services, and the adequacy of corrective institutions. The degree to which these requirements are actually met by the Family Court and related institutions sets the context within which the unit must work. The procedural modes of the court and the availability or lack of services and community-based guidance programs determine the tactics of unit attorneys and the options open to their clients. Constraints upon unit attorneys in the Family Court include the overwhelming number of cases handled by the court, the nonobservance of a number of constitutional protections normally accorded defendants when their liberty is at stake, inadequate psychiatric testing services, as well as a substantial lack of institutional facilities able to provide therapeutic guidance rather than merely custodianship. Each of these problems will be discussed in some detail inasmuch as they determine both the functions performed by the unit and the character of the representation it can offer.

Case Pressures in Family Court

The sheer volume of cases brought into the Juvenile Term of the Family Court has had a severe impact on the parole system associated with that court. According to unit attorneys, the parole system is breaking down for lack of personnel. Parole officers have been leaving and have not been replaced. As a consequence, case loads have increased to an average of 132 cases per officer. Obviously, case loads of this size make it difficult, if not impossible, for parole officers to establish personal relationships or maintain any but cursory contact with their charges. Moreover, such case pressures preclude the intensive casework many predelinquents need. Paradoxically, the strain upon the parole system works to the advantage of the Legal Unit's youthful clients. Because of the social services provided by Legal Unit social workers, offenders can be paroled directly into custody of the unit. Parole officers are often eager to have MFY accept the custody of a defendant, lightening their already overwhelming load. MFY's ability to assume parole responsibilities immediately upon the court's decision is also important. Frequently, paroled defendants must remain in detention for approximately six weeks awaiting a psychiatric examination and another four weeks before being released to supervision. For MFY parolees, this period of detention is unnecessary.[6]

Another Dimension of Case-Load Pressure: The Case of Bob and Danny

The rush of cases in the Juvenile Section of the Family Court can have unfortunate consequences for an occasional unlucky defendant. A good illustration of this problem is the case of Bob and Danny, who were accused of attempting to rob a smaller boy of his subway money. Because of the intense pressure of cases, the intake parole officer put the records of both defendants on a single sheet, and at first glance it was unclear which record was which boy's. Bob had no previous offenses, while Danny had a history of hallucinations, mental problems, and minor offenses. A mix-up occurred after Danny had been tried and exonerated. (Bob had actually made the threats.) The judge picked out the reference to hallucinations, assumed that this was Bob's record, and ordered him into immediate detention for psychiatric observation. As Bob was being led away, the unit attorney was able to point out the mistake to the intake parole officer, who helped her persuade the judge to rescind his order. Had the unit attorney not been alerted in time, or had the parole officer been uncooperative, Bob could easily have been referred to Bellevue for a long period of observation. This confusion can be traced directly to the effects of intense case-load pressures in the Family Court.

[6] An example of this was the case of Roberto R., who had slashed another student in the back with a razor. Although this was a very serious offense, he was released into the care of a unit attorney and an MFY psychiatrist. He was paroled without going to trial because MFY could offer services immediately.

The Price of Judicial Therapy

Although the intent of the Family Court in relaxing standards of evidence and formal procedures is to maximize the therapeutic effect of the experience, the practical effect is to remove a number of legal protections afforded defendants in criminal cases. The results for the defendant are often disastrous and are made still worse by the scarcity of institutional resources or community-based programs to fulfill the therapeutic purposes of the court.

By adult criminal-court standards, the practices in the Family Court are highly eccentric and in some instances illegal. A good example is the way in which accusations of rape are handled. The unit attorney who specializes in Family Court cases describes a case in which a boy was found to be a juvenile delinquent and sentenced accordingly, on the sole basis of the uncorroborated testimony of the girl involved. In criminal court, there must be medical evidence, supporting witnesses, and a doctor's testimony in support of the accusation for such a finding to be reached. Although the decision in the case mentioned above was reversed on appeal, the appeal did not reach the issue of evidentiary standards in the Family Court. Unit attorneys claim that large numbers of boys are labeled juvenile delinquents and are jailed in exactly this manner.

Another unit attorney describes a criminal case which illustrates the absence of evidentiary standards. Under normal circumstances, in a theft, the court requires the owner to identify the stolen property as his own and to prove that the defendant has possession of the property without the owner's permission. In this particular case, the defendant was accused of stealing some watches and, despite the fact that the complaining witness was unable to identify the watches as his own, was found guilty. The unit attorney objected and was offered a lesser charge and dismissal of the case if the defendant remained in school for a month. When the attorney still objected, the judge adjourned the case rather than make a ruling which then could be appealed.

While the first case was adjourned, the defendant was arrested a second time, in this instance for the theft of a typewriter. In the second case, the complaining witness was from out of town and wanted to drop the charges. The same judge refused to accept this.[7] The case was then adjourned several times and was finally settled when the judge prevailed upon the defendant's mother to accept the deal he had offered, to dismiss the second case and put the defendant on probation for the first. Had these cases been tried in adult criminal court, the charges would probably have been dropped for lack of acceptable evidence, and the judge could not have enforced his presumption of guilt on the part of the defendant.

This case also illustrates a second problem encountered in the Family Court: the tendency of the judges to act as prosecutors in the very cases they are trying. In this instance the judge refused to allow the complainant to drop the charges, and forced his decision upon the family. In another case, a judge, after convicting a Negro boy of a minor offense, asked, "By the way, what were you doing at Fifty-second and Madison anyhow?" Unit attorneys are particularly careful to keep Negro defendants away from this judge. Another judge was honest enough to admit that he disliked children and had himself transferred to Parent Relations. In general, unit attorneys avoid appearing before prejudiced or prosecuting judges by adjourning the case until a judge known to be fairer is obtained. While many judges leave much to be desired in their attitude toward defendants, according to experienced unit attorneys, many others are very good at sizing up defendants and parents alike, and deal sensitively with the difficult and often delicate human problems brought into Family Court. In part, the problem of attitude among Family Court judges could be met through more rigorous selection procedures and by requiring some special competence in an appropriate discipline—psychology, sociology, etc. According to the unit attorneys, the Family Court system has a very real need not only for more highly qualified judges

[7] Judges are not compelled to drop a charge even if the complainant withdraws his complaint. Of course the evidence is usually insufficient in the absence of a complainant.

but also for better-prepared parole officers and better-trained lawyers.

The Dilemma of New York Family Court

The primary justification for the nonlegal mode of operation of the Family Court Juvenile Term is the intention to benefit the child in a therapeutic way. However, the force of this argument is lost when the institutions and programs appropriate to a defendant's needs are lacking. Even if there were no problems of improper use of court power on the part of some judges or if the non-observance of the legal protections provided to adult criminal defendants presented no problem, the absence of alternative solutions for a child's case imposes the most severe constraint upon the therapeutic value of Family Court proceedings.

The Juvenile Term of the Family Court handles three kinds of defendants under sixteen years: (1) juvenile delinquents who have committed what would be a crime were they adults; (2) defendants defined as "persons in need of supervision" (PINS)—children accused of minor offenses, school-discipline problems, etc.; and (3) children who have been neglected, abandoned or abused by their parents.

In each type of case the court has two choices open to it: The child can be allowed to remain at home or can be placed in an institution. There are no halfway institutions which would allow the child to remain in the community or programs which would allow the child to remain at home with intensive services provided. If the child remains at home, the services provided by neighborhood settlement houses or community-service agencies are often limited to one visit a week; the possibilities of close attention and follow-up are limited, and the opportunities for deception are numerous.

The alternative is to institutionalize the child for months or years. The value of such an experience for the child is not clear. A unit attorney attempted to obtain recidivism figures from state homes and training institutions, and found that such information was not available because it had not been collected. At present there is little evidence one way or the other as to the therapeutic value of various institutional settings.

The absence of practical alternatives means that many children who could be helped in another way must be institutionalized. Unit attorneys note that such placements frequently become permanent. The limited types of institutions available to the Family Court has meant that delinquents and "persons in need of supervision" who are institutionalized are thrown in together. Children who are removed from their homes by child-neglect petitions must be institutionalized, since there is no other alternative. While there will always be a need to institutionalize the defective, emotionally disturbed, or repeatedly delinquent child, an experienced unit attorney claims that a great many more children could remain in the community or with their families if supportive services were available.[8] A unit social worker suggests that many of the present needs could be met by day-care centers and small community residential homes for teen-agers who need ties to home but also need to escape parental pressure.

The lack of community facilities and improved home-support services cannot be explained wholly in terms of cost. A unit attorney surveyed New York State detention homes, work houses, and mental hospitals, and found that 41,000 children under sixteen years were in custody, at an average annual cost of $7,300 apiece. In some families as many as five children have been removed from the home, at a yearly cost of $36,500 to the state. This unit attorney suggests that the cost of institutionalizing a single child could pay the salary of a social caseworker who could help families deal with their problems before the removal of children from the home became necessary.

Another limitation of the Family Court is the lack of adequate

[8] A good example of this is the case of Nora P. who, though mentally defective, was capable of caring for her children. The children had been removed from the home on a child-neglect petition due to the disorganization and unsanitary condition of the home. Unit attorneys took up her case, obtained the release of the children, and provided follow-up support. At the present time, she is maintaining her family quite well.

psychiatric-testing services directly available to the court. If a judge has an obviously psychotic defendant before him, he has little choice: He can risk returning the child to the community, remand him to Bellevue, or take his chances with the limited diagnostic resources at hand. Unit attorneys representing clients with mental problems try to ensure that their trials are scheduled for the morning, when the psychiatric clinic is available.

The Role of the Social Worker

The social and legal services provided by the Legal Unit compensate in part for the lack of community resources for family problems. As already noted, the ability of the unit to provide on-going support services for the individual juvenile defendant has enabled MFY in many cases to obtain parole custody of a defendant and thereby prevent his institutionalization. Similarly, the presence of an MFY social worker has frequently enabled families faced with child-neglect petitions to retain the custody of their children.

A unit attorney who appeared in thirty Family Court cases over a three-month period reports that only one child was placed in an institution while two others were held temporarily. Some of the cases involved families with several children who would have been removed from the home and placed in institutions. Thus, the number of children which could have been institutionalized was significantly greater than thirty. The contribution of supportive social services to the effectiveness of the legal representation provided by the unit is indicated by this attorney's estimate that one third of the children would have been lost to institutions without social-service support. The social-service component of the unit does provide the kind of community-based service not otherwise available.

The social workers attached to the unit are an important source of referrals to the lawyers at the point of the client's difficulty with a governmental agency or a private individual or a business organization. However, the most important functions performed by unit social workers are in relation to the actual work of the attorneys in Family Court cases. An MFY memorandum describes the social worker's role as one in which he . . .

> . . . explores the family situation, provides crisis intervention at the point of the family's confrontation with the court, works with extended-family relationships, works to develop the most desirable resources for the family, etc. The worker tries to help the family mobilize its strengths and develop its own plans for dealing with its problems. The lawyer and social worker may then bring this plan to the court. Often, the court will accept such a plan as alternative to the use of authority.

Unit social workers maintain contact with the clients and assist them in their dealings with public agencies.

> . . . another major function of the Social Service Unit has been in the visiting and accompanying of clients to various institutions of the city, either to serve in the capacity of a witness in court, or to give the client support in what might be a stressful situation; or to interview an individual who might be out of the home . . . and [this is] important for the lawyer in that the social worker can keep him appraised of important developments in the case.

Where necessary, unit social workers will relate to a family on a casework basis. In one case daily contact was needed to restructure the family relationship to keep six children in the home. Unit social workers also provide the attorneys with important insights, analyses of a family's problems, and suggested solutions. Some attorneys use the social worker as a sounding board to test out strategies in a case, as well as for advice.

There have, however, been instances of conflict between attorneys and Legal Unit social workers, most of them arising from differing professional ethics. The lawyer's first duty is to protect his client's legal rights and best interests; social workers attempt to work out the best solution for *all* the concerned parties. Conflict therefore arises when the attorney represents the parents in a neglect proceeding, and the children also need help. In such cases the social workers will remain out of the court presentation of the case. Nevertheless, the inclusion of the social worker in the process of providing legal counsel to troubled families has been essential to the success of the unit with Family Court cases.

Representation of Indigent Parents in Neglect Proceedings

An important function of the Legal Unit is to provide counsel to indigent parents in child-neglect proceedings and to represent indigent men brought before the court for failure to meet alimony or support payments. In the latter type of case, the defendant usually cannot afford an attorney; when asked if he wants an adjournment of the case to obtain representation, he will often reject the adjournment. He is then liable to receive a six-months' sentence for contempt of court on the original order to pay support. Unit attorneys hope to get the court to accept the state's responsibility for providing legal assistance to indigent defendants when the court intends to impose a prison sentence.

In child-neglect cases, unit representation of the indigent parents serves to protect them against petitions initiated on an unreasonable basis or without proper cause. By defeating the neglect action, the unit maintains the integrity of the family; it can then provide supplementary social assistance to help the family with its problems.

A recent case illustrates how neglect actions based on inaccurate information can threaten to break up a family unnecessarily. In this instance a seventeen-year-old girl had complained of sexual advances by her father. She had called in a Society for the Prevention of Cruelty to Children investigator who, after a month of visiting the family, initiated a child-neglect petition to have the children removed from the home. Upon investigation by unit social workers, it became clear that the girl's stories were fantasies and that she had been sexually playing with her younger brother. The unit attorney attempted to settle the case out of court, but the Society for the Prevention of Cruelty to Children investigator insisted on going to court. In the process of the trial, the fantasy basis of the girl's allegations was brought out. As a consequence, the neglect action was dropped, and the girl was placed under psychiatric observation. Nevertheless, the experience was very hard on the family.

In this case the Society for the Prevention of Cruelty to Children worker had misdiagnosed the situation with terrible effects for the family. Had the parents appeared without counsel, the children could easily have been removed from the home unjustly and the family's home life completely destroyed. The unit attorneys indicate that it is difficult to win a neglect case without competent legal assistance, since Family Court judges are generally disposed to accept an investigator's argument supporting the neglect petition and are easily convinced that she knows what's best for the family. In these situations the importance of counsel for the parents becomes clear. The attorney will ask questions, probe the responses for more facts, test the credibility of the testimony, and expose inconsistencies in the evidence or argument supporting the neglect action. In sum, unit representation of indigent parents can help to protect them against an unequal, unfair encounter with the law.

Conclusions

The work of the Legal Unit has served to reduce discretionary and discriminatory effects of the Family Court system. It also compensates in part for the absence of community institutions for delinquent and predelinquent youth. In doing so, the unit in effect increases the options available to the court and the defendant by providing opportunities for supervision aside from sending the defendant home or having him placed in an institution. Moreover, the detailed service and social-service follow-up has resulted in placements better suited to the needs of the defendant.

By joining social service with legal advocacy, the unit has provided certain necessary resources so that judicial determinations can more sensitively reflect the needs of the defendant. In short, unit representation helps the Family Court system to fulfill its therapeutic goal more effectively than would otherwise be possible within the constraints set by informal court procedure, discretion of the judges, case-load pressures, and the lack of institutional or program resources for the noncriminal defendant.

4

Caveat Emptor: Legal Assistance to the Unwary Consumer

Michael Appleby

Approximately 10 percent of the cases brought to the MFY Legal Services Unit involve a consumer-related problem.[1] Experience with this area of the law reflects conditions endemic to all urban areas: an immobile, uninformed (as to comparative prices, legal rights, etc.), and apathetic low-income market, confronted by slum merchants adept in sharp business practices and in the manipulation of the law to the serious disadvantage of the low-income consumer.[2] A brief introduction to the problems encountered by the low-income consumer will provide some perspective for the experience of the Legal Services Unit.

Credit and the Poor

The most serious legal problems a low-income consumer faces have to do with credit purchases.[3] Ready credit has brought the

[1] The actual number of consumer cases was 546 out of a total case load of 5,785 from January 1964 to May 1967.

[2] For a full discussion of the low-income consumer's problems, see David Caplovitz, *The Poor Pay More* (New York, The Free Press of Glencoe, 1963).

[3] The fact that low-income consumers are consistently offered goods at higher prices than middle-income consumers pay also poses grave problems, but since this form of economic discrimination does not raise legal issues,

67

low-income consumer into the market for formerly unobtainable goods. Thus a survey of five hundred low-income families in lower Manhattan found that 95 percent of the respondents owned a television set, 60 percent a phonograph, and 40 percent a sewing machine, and that over 50 percent had spent $500 or more on furniture sets.[4] Credit arrangements for these families were crucial: Eighty percent of the families had used credit to purchase some durable goods; two thirds of the durables owned by these families had been bought on credit, and 60 percent of the families had debts outstanding.

The study also found that most of the purchases had been made from neighborhood merchants or door-to-door salesmen. Both types of slum merchants are willing to extend credit to poor risks because they can charge exorbitant credit rates and high mark-ups on low-quality merchandise. They can then transfer their debts to collection agencies, which rely on garnishment of wages. Over one fifth of the families surveyed reported having experienced some form of pressure related to difficulties in keeping up installment-contract payments. Such pressures included threats, repossession of the goods, and salary garnishments. Many low-income consumers do not understand the consequences of failure to maintain the payments of an installment loan, and few of them anticipate the difficulty of keeping up the payments. Often other possessions—television sets, furniture, etc.—can be repossessed in lieu of or in addition to the object in question. Often the wages of the head of the household will be garnished to recover the debt. Many em-

---

it is beyond the scope of this paper. A MFY comparison of supermarket and small-shop prices in the Lower East Side and in middle-class areas of Manhattan found that for equal amounts of staples—sugar, soup, flour, milk, beans, etc.—the Lower East Side shopper paid 9.4 percent more than a shopper in a comparison middle-class area and 20 percent more than a shopper in a cooperative market. See the chapter on "Consumer Affairs Programs" in Vol. 2, *Community Development,* for a full discussion of this problem.

[4] David Caplovitz, "Consumer Problems," Conference Proceedings, The Extension of Legal Services to the Poor (Washington, D.C., Department of Health, Education and Welfare, 1964), p. 62.

ployers, unwilling to go to the trouble of garnishing a menial worker's salary, will fire him instead.

Compounding the effects of lack of knowledge or foresight on
the part of the consumer are the sales strategies of slum merchants.
Questionable practices are typical: deliberately misrepresenting an
item's actual price by not including taxes, interest charges, and
fees; switch sales, in which second-rate goods advertised at extremely low prices are used to lure customers into the store, where
they are then pressured into buying better-quality goods at much
higher prices; selling reconditioned goods as new; general high-
pressure sales techniques; never allowing exchanges; etc. Customers who intend to pay cash often become credit customers after
being talked into buying more expensive items than they had
originally wanted. Slum merchants are able to capitalize on what
Caplovitz calls compensatory consumption—the desire for tangible
status symbols to compensate for blocked mobility.[5]

The operation of the law regulating installment contracts poses
another problem for the low-income consumer. The Caplovitz
survey found that many purchasers, unaware of the consequences,
often simply stopped making payments when they found that they
had been cheated.[6] By taking the initiative in this way, the consumer becomes subject to legal sanctions for repossession of the
goods or wage garnishment. Moreover, the low-income buyer often
has little idea of where to obtain assistance with legal problems
which arise out of credit obligations. Caplovitz found that only a
small number of the families surveyed mention the Better Business
Bureau as a possible source of help and only 3 percent mentioned
going to a lawyer.[7]

Not only is the law structured in favor of the merchant, but the
way in which it is applied also works to the disadvantage of the
low-income consumer. In a great number of cases, even those in
which the consumer is willing to defend the case, the first sign that
legal action is being taken is the notice of wage garnishment.

[5] *Ibid.*, p. 63.
[6] Caplovitz, *The Poor Pay More, op. cit.*, p. 13.
[7] Caplovitz, "Consumer Problems," *op. cit.*, p. 64.

Notices which would alert the consumer are often simply not delivered by the merchant's attorney or the city marshal. As a consequence, a judgment of default is entered since no defense has been offered, and the consumer faces repossession or garnishment. Even when notice is received, frequently the low-income consumer cannot afford to risk his precarious employment by attending time-consuming court hearings. All things considered, the law, as Caplovitz puts it, acts as the unwitting collection agent for the merchant.[8]

The already disadvantaged situation of the low-income consumer is often further complicated by the practice, common among slum merchants, of selling installment contracts to collection agencies. This has the effect of making the merchant less responsible to his customer, pitting the consumer against an organization which has no market relationship to maintain in the neighborhood and can afford to use unethical tactics to recover the debt. Here, as in other areas of poverty law, the contending parties are far from equal. The often ill-informed, vulnerable, low-income consumer must defend himself against threats and manipulations of the law by an experienced collection agency. Here, as in other areas, the net effect of the operation of the law, because of lost jobs, reduced income, and increased debt for the low-income consumer, is to force him deeper into poverty and increase his disrespect for law.[9]

The Abuse of Legal Process

In consumer affairs, one of the Legal Unit's primary interests became the extent to which the requirements of legal process in the recovery of debts were being systematically bypassed by the collection agencies. Just as with landlord-tenant eviction proceedings, "sewer service" or the nondelivery of court notices appeared to be widely practiced. The initial evidence of sewer service of court process was provided by the clients themselves. Unit attorneys estimated that 95 percent of their consumer-fraud cases involved

[8] *Ibid.*
[9] Caplovitz, *The Poor Pay More, op. cit.*

clients for whom the first indication of court action being taken against them was an attachment to their wages.

As a consistent pattern emerged, the Legal Unit initiated a study of default judgments obtained by the retail stores, companies, and collection agencies which had most often been connected with cases brought into the unit. The study was to consist of two parts: a search of court records of default judgments obtained, and interviews with those who had received the judgments.

The unit first drew up a list of the stores, agencies, lawyers, etc., who had been "implicated at least once in a case of alleged non-service of process." [10] Next, MFY lawyers examined the records of legal actions brought by the listed firms and attorneys in the civil courts of New York and Kings counties for the months of July and August 1964. In the Civil Court of New York alone, 540 actions were brought in the two-month period. Of these 532 had resulted in default judgments; only eight had been defended.[11] Not all the firms or attorneys with whom the Legal Unit had had consumer-related litigations brought a legal action during that two-month period. One notable exception was an attorney who had opposed unit attorneys in many consumer cases. It was found that this attorney brought his cases in Brooklyn rather than New York Civil Court, and a random sample of a hundred of his cases produced the following:

100 percent of the judgments were entered by default;
60 percent of the cases involved improper venue, neither plaintiff nor defendant being a Brooklyn resident;
6 percent of the judgments had been subsequently voided;

[10] "Memorandum: Mobilization For Youth Default Study" (mimeographed, New York, Mobilization For Youth, September 1, 1965), p. 1.

[11] *Ibid.*, p. 2. The following quote illustrates the magnitude of the problem: "A study of the docket books in the New York County Civil Court by the CORE Legal Department showed that in 1964, some twelve companies brought 30,000 cases against consumers; 28,000 of these went to judgment and 27,500 or 99 percent went to default judgment. Since several highly reputable firms were included in these twelve companies, these figures are no doubt representative of all consumer cases." "Default Judgments in Consumer Actions: The Survey of Defendants" (mimeographed, New York, Mobilization For Youth, 1965), p. 1.

this attorney's litigation comprised approximately 25 percent of all cases brought in the Brooklyn Civil Court.[12]

The second stage of the study called for interviews with three hundred defendants in the default-judgment cases studied. Unfortunately, however, the great majority of respondents selected were no longer living at the addresses indicated in the court records, and the volunteer interviewers were unable to track them down. As a consequence, only thirty usable interviews were obtained. While such a small sample is not authoritative, the results are nevertheless suggestive.

Of the thirty respondents, twenty-six earned less than $4,000 annually; three earned between $4,000 and $5,000, and one earned more than $5,000 a year. The respondents were asked about the details of purchase and the legal actions taken against them. Special care was taken to ascertain whether the respondent had received the several court notices which precede and accompany a default judgment. Copies of the relevant court's paper were shown to each respondent to assure the reliability of the response. As already noted, most of the unit's clients in consumer cases learned of the legal action against them only when their wages had been garnished. For this to happen, several legal procedures in which the defendant is to be notified of the impending legal action must be violated.

The first step in the process is a court hearing, for which the defendant must receive a summons. About one third of those interviewed reported receiving such a summons. After the default judgment has been entered, the defendant is to receive a notice of the judgment. As with the court summons, two thirds of the respondents reported, after being shown a sample, that they never received the notice of default judgment. Finally, three quarters of the respondents reported income executions against them. The defendant, according to the law, is to receive a notice of the income execution twenty days before the deductions are to begin, to give him an opportunity to settle the debt before his wages are attached.

[12] *Ibid.*, p. 4.

Only one in four of those whose wages had been attached reported receiving such a notice.

The survey suggests that the companies involved systematically ignored the requirements of legal process, with the result that most defendants remained unaware of (and therefore unable to defend against) the legal action being taken against them. In the majority of cases, the summons to court hearing, the notice of default judgment, and the notice of an income execution were not delivered to the defendant. As the author of the study puts it, by this time "it is often too late for the consumer to protect his job, much less his legal rights, in the action taken against him." [13]

In addition, contrary to the popular belief that the poor fail to pay their debts because they are irresponsible or dishonest, the survey found that the majority of the respondents had withheld payments in response to consumer fraud on the part of the merchant.

> The consumer would find that the merchandise cost much more than he was led to believe it would at the time he signed the contract, or he would find the merchandise delivered was not the merchandise he ordered, or he would discover that the merchandise was damaged in some way.[14]

The Experience of the Legal Unit

One unit client paid over $400 for an old-fashioned type of washing machine which normally costs $80 at retail prices. Another unit client paid $1,148 for a freezer unit which costs $348 at retail prices. In such cases, where the exorbitant overcharge is obvious, unit attorneys are able to rely upon a recently incorporated clause of the New York State Uniform Commercial Code which provides the consumer with a defense against "unconscionable profits." [15]

[13] "Default Judgments in Consumer Actions: The Survey of Defendants," *op. cit.*, p. 9.
[14] *Ibid.*, p. 10.
[15] Uniform Commercial Code, State of New York, Section 2 302.

Contracts where the doctrine of unconscionable profits applies can be voided in court. While this does provide some protection, the low-income consumer still remains on the defensive, since most cases are brought to the unit after a default judgment has been entered and wage attachment initiated. As a consequence, unit attorneys enter a case at a serious disadvantage. Reopening the case involves a lengthy process.

To the consumer who lacks legal representation, the collection agents are extremely threatening. In one instance, for example, a Puerto Rican woman was told that she and her children would be jailed if her debt was not paid. However, after an attorney for the consumer-defendant enters the case and petitions the court to reopen the default judgment, the attitude of the collection agent quickly changes, and the issue begins to be worked out. When the doctrine of unconscionable profit clearly applies or when false claims can be substantiated, the claim may be dropped or the debt reduced.

Although in a few cases the contracts have not been vulnerable to a legal challenge, the general response to the intervention of unit attorneys has been one of accommodation. The collection agents have been agreeable and cooperative. It is conceivable, as one unit attorney suggests, that the collection agencies would put up stiff legal resistance were the unit cases to become part of a larger trend. The absence of legal resistance may be due in part to the small number of cases handled by the unit in relation to the very large numbers of cases initiated by the most active firms. In a three-and-a-half-year period, for example, the Legal Services Unit provided assistance in 541 consumer cases. As already noted, for 1964 alone in one county court, the twelve most active firms accounted for 27,500 default judgments.

Perhaps, with the organization of neighborhood legal offices throughout the New York area, a rising volume of defended default actions might begin to curtail the most exploitative practices. Perhaps merely a higher incidence of defenses will accomplish what a large volume would: the inducement of more lawful behavior among slum merchants. One observer suggests that a randomness

in legal defenses might restrain some of the most fraudulent
behavior:

> One of the great advantages of asserting private rights, from the
> standpoint of inducing persons to conduct themselves lawfully, is the
> randomness of private litigation. . . . If a legal assistance program
> can establish a climate among the poor in which individuals begin
> asserting their rights against unconscionable conduct, the conse-
> quences will be to make suppliers of credit proceed more cautiously
> and within the boundaries of conscionable conduct. . . . The supplier
> will then be faced with the inability of predicting when an individual
> will challenge him with unconscionable conduct.[16]

However, the creation of this atmosphere poses serious problems. The experience of the Legal Unit indicates that part of the
answer must lie in the education of the consumer to recognize a
legal problem when it arises or the immediate need for legal assistance so that the problem will not arise. Even more important,
he must learn to avoid becoming entangled in improper credit
relationships from the first. The latter is perhaps more easily ac-
complished than the former. When a consumer finds that his wages
have been attached or feels that he has been cheated, referral of
the problem to a lawyer would seem to be a fairly obvious solution. Nevertheless, unit attorneys report that consumers frequently
feel that they are at fault for letting themselves be cheated and
deserve to pay in full. They are unwilling to admit that they have
been tricked. Moreover, the well-documented fatalism of the poor
is another obstacle which must be overcome if fraudulent sales
behavior is to be subjected to consistent legal scrutiny. The availability of legal counsel in itself is no guarantee that scrutiny will
be brought to bear in situations where it might be appropriate.

Consumer education, in addition to the availability of legal resources, can be helpful in reducing exploitative sales. However,
consumer-education programs are of limited effectiveness, because

[16] Allison Dunham, "Consumer Credit Problems of the Poor—Legal Assistance as an Aid in Law Reform," Conference Proceedings (Washington,
D.C. National Conference on Law and Poverty, June 1965), p. 12.

it is precisely the person who most needs such educational help who is least likely to attend consumer clinics. This would include the people who are unable to get to such meetings, those who feel that nothing can be done to avoid being cheated, and those who, because of their lack of sophistication or experience, simply fail to perceive the need for such programs.[17] While consumer education is an important part of an overall program, the programs can hardly be considered a panacea. As long as there is an intense desire on the part of the poor to share in the affluent society, and as long as there are unscrupulous merchants, there will be victims of fraud and a need for readily available legal counsel.

Another method of attacking unscrupulous commercial practices would be to reform the State Commercial Code. The Legal Unit made one attempt at legislative reform. With the cooperation of the New York attorney general, the unit proposed legislation which would put an end to sewer service by creating a state licensing procedure, a systematic review of marshals' activities, and criminal penalties for perjury in giving evidence concerning the delivery of court processes.[18] The proposal, however, was rejected by the state legislature.

Conclusions

Because the Commercial Code is based on the "buyer beware" principle, the consumer is at a serious disadvantage. The code makes it the buyer's responsibility to detect overpricing, exorbitant credit rates, and phony claims, and to resist high-pressure salesmen. Although it is incumbent upon the seller to observe com-

---

[17] Mobilization For Youth sponsored consumer clinics and found it was, in general, the most sophisticated consumer who participated in the programs. Those who needed the help most were the most difficult to reach. After 1965 the consumer clinics were discontinued because of lack of funding. However, the Legal Services Unit held consumer-education clinics with local groups from time to time.

[18] The Legal Unit drew up an act whose purpose was "to amend the general business law and the civil practices law and rules in relation to providing for the licensing and regulation of persons engaged in the business of serving process."

mercial regulatory codes, in the absence of adequate enforcement of the codes an unscrupulous businessman has little incentive to do so. He can transfer the debt, and the collection agent can garnishee. Several unit lawyers suggest that the commercial codes be rewritten to give the consumer greater protection from exploitative sales conduct, particularly by abolishing garnishment and providing assurances that processes are served. The Legal Unit could contribute to such a reformulation, but it has few resources with which to initiate it. At best, the unit can propose legislation, but it can do little to press for the political acceptance of its proposals.

In dealing with consumer-fraud cases, the unit provides a service to the client by challenging the legal action taken against him. Moreover, the unit's activities on the Lower East Side—the clients represented, the consumer clinics held—contribute to the creation of a more knowledgeable community. However, beyond providing service to the victims of fraud and offering some consumer education to the community, there is little the unit can do to challenge the basic legislative context which permits the commercial abuses described here. Without organized consumer groups which can exert political pressure for legislative reform (at which point the unit could contribute its experience to the process of evaluating the code), the unit can do little more than protect individual consumers against being defrauded.

Yet, the fact that legal assistance for consumer problems exists in the neighborhood represents a significant contribution, providing the poor with an additional resource to oppose injustices associated with their poverty. When collection agencies realize that they will be opposed in court, they tend to settle to avoid court costs. The fact of opposition is an important determinant in the fight to see that low-income consumers are treated fairly. An unforeseen consequence of the tendency of vendors or their agents to settle out of court, however, has been the inability of the unit to bring test cases to challenge the consumer legislative codes. Most of the cases are settled out of court.

Should legal services for the poor consumer become increasingly available, not only may vendors and their agents become less exploitative, but the laws under which they operate may be more stringently scrutinized by the courts. This may ultimately lead to the courts' insistence on due process and basic legislative reform.

5

Legal Enforcement of Laws Affecting Private Housing

Michael Appleby and Harold H. Weissman

A prime factor which conditions the operation of housing laws is that the poor, because of their low economic status, must choose from a limited stock of the oldest, most deteriorated housing available. Moreover, the low-income housing supply is continually being reduced as new highways and urban-renewal projects invade slum housing areas. The supply of public housing being far from sufficient, the poor have little choice but to live wherever they can find cheap accommodation.

Another factor which affects the operation of housing laws relates to the economics of housing. The costs of repairing many of the dilapidated tenements in slum areas like the Lower East Side are prohibitive for many landlords, especially for those who are undercapitalized and have little skill in building management. Thus pressure exists on landlords not to make repairs so that they can keep their profit margin. In cases involving the enforcement of housing laws, the courts tend to be sympathetic to the economic needs of landlords. In addition, the fact that there is an insufficient supply of housing for the poor without doubt raises questions in the minds of judges sympathetic to tenant problems as to where tenants would live if economically unstable landlords were forced out of business. Who would buy the buildings and make the needed repairs? In this context of pressures operating on courts, landlords, and tenants alike, the Legal Unit case load of tenant–private landlord disputes rose regularly over the years, averaging seventy a month during 1967. This paper will examine the effects of providing legal counsel to the tenants.

As in other areas of poverty law, legal principles which support the low-income tenant are quite underdeveloped. This is the result of the fact that historically the low-income tenant has not had access to legal resources and has thus been unable to assert his legal interests or to compel the development of his side of property law.[1]

The tenant's disadvantage is compounded by the complex procedures and the multiplicity of courts and departments that administer housing law. For example, until 1965, New York City had five departments with nineteen subdivisions handling housing complaints. Those tenants who braved the bureaucratic intricacies of code-enforcement agencies frequently had to wait several months for a housing inspection. Besides the delay and red tape which inhibited the tenant's efforts to assert his housing rights, landlords received absurdly low fines for permitting serious housing violations in their properties. In 1964, the average fine administered under Section 304 of the Multiple Dwelling Law was only $16.[2]

In reference to criminal summonses issued to landlords an observer noted, "The court where the summons is returnable tends to see its office as a kind of mediation-counseling service . . . and strives to adjust and compromise situations. . . ."[3] The reluctance of the court to prosecute landlords requires tenants to persist through numerous hearings, adjournments, and continuances. Such

[1] For a discussion of the general lack of adequate development in poor man's law, see Jerome Carlin, Jan Howard, and Sheldon Messinger, "Civil Justice and the Poor," *Law and Society,* Vol. 1, No. 1 (February 1966), Center for the Study of Law and Society, University of California at Berkeley, pp. 17–21.

[2] Patricia M. Wald, "Law and Poverty: 1965" (Washington, D.C., National Conference on Law and Poverty, June 1965), p. 15.

[3] Nancy LeBlanc, "Landlord-Tenant Problems," Conference Proceedings, The Extension of Legal Services to the Poor (Washington, D.C., Department of Health, Education and Welfare, 1964), p. 67.

repeated appearances in court constitute a form of harassment for the low-income tenant.

> It works out that the tenant must come to court innumerable times. Each time he must again tell the judge what his complaints are and what the landlord has or has not done to satisfy the complaint since last time they were in court. This may go on for months with progress at a snail's pace so that, in the end, the tenant may well wonder if it was all worth it.[4]

The tenant's disadvantage is further compounded by the general disregard of the required procedures through which he is supposed to be notified of impending actions against him. Often the first indication a tenant receives of summary eviction proceedings is a notice from a city marshal that he has to quit the premises within twenty-four hours. In such cases the landlord has made use of sewer service, simply ignoring the required niceties of posting a copy on the tenant's door and mailing a copy to him. The tenant's only choice is to capitulate or to prove in court that no letter of notification was received. Such a defense would be impossible without the aid of a lawyer.

Despite the many instances in which the law as written and administered is biased against the tenant, New York City housing legislation is probably the most liberal in the country in affording the low-income tenant means by which he can pursue his legal right to a safe and sanitary dwelling.[5] But while legislation helps to equalize the forces in the encounter between landlord and tenant, much of this legislation goes unenforced, and much has little pertinence to low-income tenants because skilled legal representation

[4] *Ibid.*, p. 57.

[5] Section 2040 Penal Law Summons permits a tenant to take out a criminal summons against a landlord who has failed to provide essential services. Section 755 of the Real Property Action Proceedings Law allows the tenant to pay rent to the court and to arrange for repairs to be paid out of the rent money. There are also laws pertaining to rent abatement and rent strikes.

has not been available. The absence of counsel underlies the ineffectiveness of housing legislation.

Almost all tenant remedies involve a formal court appearance, requiring adherence to rigorous standards of evidence, official records of violations, and other complex legal procedures. For his part, the landlord will attack the evidence and put forth justifying arguments. These facts make it necessary that the tenant have an attorney to represent him. It is not the lack of legislation but the unavailability of lawyers to enforce it which allows dangerous and degrading housing conditions to persist.

Activities and Accomplishments of the Legal Unit

Most of the private-housing cases handled by the Legal Unit can be divided into three categories: (1) obtaining the services paid for—heat, hot water, etc.; (2) having needed repairs made; and (3) reversing eviction for nonpayment of rent, usually because of the loss of a job or a late welfare or pay check. The remedies now most frequently utilized by the unit attorneys are the 755 order and the Article 7-A proceeding regarding rent strikes.

The criminal summons is used occasionally when quick results are needed and there is a single major source to the problems—for example, in connection with the provision of heat, electricity, or water. The value of Section 2040 lies in the shock it gives a landlord to be served with a criminal summons. If quick results are not forthcoming and the action threatens to become drawn out into a series of hearings, the one legal action open to the tenant is a 755 order, which stipulates that the violations amount to a "constructive eviction of the tenant."

The effect of legal counsel on housing laws was especially evident during the rent-strike movement of 1964.[6] Both the 2040 criminal summons and the 755 order were unknown and unused before the rent strikes. Both were then applied with some success. By uncovering these forgotten statutes, attorneys defending the

[6] See the chapter "The Housing Program, 1962 to 1967" in Vol. 2, *Community Development,* for a detailed description of this movement.

rent strikes opened an avenue for the striking tenants' demands. Without these legal defenses, it is certain that fewer improvements would have been made, the strikers would not have been sustained as long as they were, and sizable numbers of strikers would have been evicted.

The effect of the rent strike extended beyond the immediate improvements obtained for the striking tenants, although these were considerable. (During a three-month period in 1964 the unit represented 175 rent-strike cases.) The conditions exposed by the strikers created a ground swell of public indignation and support for housing reforms. The results were bills which authorized expansion of conditions under which rent strikes are legal (Article 7-A proceeding), a complete abatement of rent under certain conditions (Section 302-A, multiple-dwelling law), and an amendment to the 755 order which permits a complaining tenant to arrange and pay for repairs out of funds deposited with the courts.[7]

Since the passage of Article 7-A, whicn sets forth the guidelines for a rent strike, the use of the 755 order in general has changed. In 1964 a 755 order was the defense for the nonpayment of rent in cases where the requirements of Article 7-A had not been fulfilled. The 755 order is always available as a last-resort defense for the tenant who is willing to confront the landlord on the conditions of the building but is unable to secure the cooperation of the one third of the tenants necessary to institute an Article 7-A proceeding.

A basic function of the 755 order is to protect the tenant from being thrown out on the street while at the same time exposing the violations in the building. The defense against eviction is especially important in cases where the marshal fails to notify the tenant. A Legal Unit study exposed this practice, showing that such sewer service was a frequent occurrence.

The provision of legal counsel, in addition to providing tangible protection and relief to tenants, had more subtle effects. An important lesson of the Legal Unit's experience in housing law relates

[7] For an argument that stresses the limitations of legal procedures in rent strikes see the chapter on "The Housing Program, 1962 to 1967" in Vol. 2, *Community Development*.

to the role of law as a structure for landlord-tenant relationships. The provision of legal counsel for tenants essentially was based on the tenet that an individual has no rights, no protection under a rule of law, unless he has some means of enforcing the law and asserting his rights. Legislation provides a structure for the inter-action of landlords and tenants by defining rights and obligations, and specifying expectations. The activities of the Legal Unit have helped to create a climate in which the tenant is no longer so dependent upon the good will of the landlord; the tenant now has a greater capability for supporting or asserting his housing interest through the law, and his position is consequently less defensive.

When the Legal Unit first represented low-income tenants in housing matters, it met stiff landlord resistance and hostility from the courts. Landlords fought each case without compromise. One attorney went so far as to attack the unit's free representation of low-income tenants on constitutional grounds. Although the case was dismissed, it is illustrative of the resistance generated by the unit's activities. Since that time, however, a real change has oc-curred in attitudes and landlord response. In the first place, the Legal Unit has become very well-known to landlords and the courts alike. Much of the hostility was apparently based on a mis-understanding of MFY goals.[8] As time passed it was clear that the unit was fighting for the rights of tenants under the law and that unit attorneys did not easily relinquish the defense of low-income clients' interests.

Secondly, with the passage of new housing legislation and an accumulation of unit experience, an important change took place in the response of landlords. Whereas landlords originally fought each issue as far as the legal process would allow, today they usually agree quickly to make the needed repairs. In housing, as in other kinds of cases, the threat of litigation is a powerful pres-sure for settlement out of court. Landlords have recognized that a

[8] This occurred during the time when MFY was under public attack by a variety of interests opposed to its goals. See the paper "The Attack on Mobilization" in Vol. 2, *Community Development,* for a description of these events.

court defense is very costly and that they are likely to lose. (The Legal Unit has won every Article 7-A proceeding it has entered.) As a consequence an estimated seven out of ten Article 7-A proceedings are settled out of court or in the early stages of litigation. The same is true of cases involving 755 orders. Few cases actually go to court now. The change from intense resistance to prompt negotiation of settlement is perhaps the most dramatic instance of social change effected through the efforts of the Legal Unit.

Conclusions

Despite the fact that landlords have become more responsive to their tenants' housing needs as defined by law, enforcement of present housing legislation is not a panacea for the housing problems of the area. Cases are won, repairs are made, and violations removed without effecting any broad changes. So long as the fundamental material conditions of the old buildings remain as they are, legal action on behalf of tenants will continue to be remedial, crisis-oriented, and repetitive. What results then is a patchwork of repairs, stopgap solutions, and crisis-oriented action. While the worst conditions can be bettered and tenants' immediate needs met, the general deterioration of an old, outmoded, and vulnerable housing stock continues.

The conflict between the cost of essential repairs and the ability of poor tenants to pay for them is the central dilemma of housing reform. Strict code-enforcement programs and various rehabilitation schemes all suffer from the same serious defect of raising the cost of housing beyond an acceptable point for low-income tenants.[9] This problem is illustrated by the unit's experience with Article 7-A proceedings. Before the law had been used to any extent, it was feared that the rent money in some cases would be insufficient

[9] In most jurisdictions, another major limitation on the ability of tenants to exercise their legal rights is the failure to have any control over eviction. In New York City rent control serves two major functions: It controls the amount of rent, and it controls the right of the landlord to evict. In many slum areas landlords rent to tenants on a month-to-month basis, so that at the end of any month they may evict the tenant without cause since the lease has expired—in effect a retaliatory eviction.

to finance the needed repairs. Another fear was that the administrator might be collecting rent for years and have to use repair
money for janitorial services, emergency repairs, etc.

These fears were confirmed in a recent Article 7-A proceeding
in which a Legal Unit attorney was appointed court administrator
to oversee the repair of a building. A local social worker agreed to
collect rent and arrange repairs. Soon after the appointment of the
unit attorney as court administrator, the boiler broke down and
cost $300 to fix. Other costs—normal maintenance, fuel bills,
etc.—mounted up. To date the building has cost more to operate
than it has produced in rent money. To meet these costs the administrator has been forced to arrange deferred payment with a
fuel company. At the present time the removal of major violations
which occasioned the Article 7-A proceedings is out of the question.[10]

Although this case may not be typical, it does illustrate some of
the dilemmas involved in winning improved living conditions for
low-income tenants. It is clear that a greater public commitment
to provide adequate housing for poor people is required. Despite
the impressive achievements of the Legal Unit in private-housing
law, the need for more housing is greater than the need for new
legislation. At the same time, the societal attitude toward the need
for adequate housing must itself change. In the words of Legal Unit
attorney Nancy LeBlanc:

> If the right to shelter is recognized as a basic right which should
> be guaranteed to all persons, then we might begin to think of hous-

[10] ". . . there is pending a proposal to amend Article 7-A to allow the
appropriate department of the city government to be appointed administrator. This had real possibilities since the city has greater resources to
draw upon in performing and carrying out the functions of administrator.
Also, the city, under separate legislation, has the right to make emergency
repairs in property and to place a lien against the rent for such repairs.
Therefore the city might be able to put up more money immediately for
repairs than would be possible for the administrator who must depend
solely on the monthly rent." Nancy LeBlanc, "Tenants Need New Laws to
Insure Their Equity," *Virginia Law Weekly,* Vol. 20, No. 16 (February 29,
1968), p. 2.

ing as a form of public utility subject to the same kind of controls imposed upon other public utilities, such as electricity, gas, and telephone. Therefore the law must develop to protect the public against the arbitrary and capricious acts of those private profit makers who have control over a service or facility which is considered essential to the well-being and life of all people. . . . It is my belief that it is only as we begin to move toward the concept of housing as a public utility that we can begin to balance the right of tenants versus landlords and to grant to the indigent tenant some security in his home while affording him remedies for asserting his right to have his home properly maintained and repaired at all times.[11]

[11] *Ibid.,* p. 4.

6

Legal Challenges to Formal and Informal Denials of Welfare Rights

Michael Appleby and Henry Heifetz

The New York welfare system is by now so refined that it allots forty-nine bobby pins a year to every unemployed woman and nine haircuts to every unemployed man. There is no such precision in the definition of the rights of its clients; they are ruled by the discretion of welfare workers who, in the best of cases, are under continual reminder to keep costs down.[1]

In the New York Welfare Department strict accounting and official pressure to spend the least amount possible, often regardless of the human consequences, lead easily to conflict between welfare worker and client. In many areas of welfare law, legislation is vaguely written and standards are poorly defined. Consequently the individual welfare worker has considerable discretionary power. The high yearly rate of staff turnover (30 percent) in New York's Department of Welfare also means that an inexperienced welfare worker may not know the law which he is responsible for administering.

When the law is not explicit, the nature of the relationship between the client and the welfare worker becomes especially important. A worker's dislike for a client is easily translated into

[1] Sherman Barr, "Poverty on the Lower East Side" (mimeographed, New York, Mobilization For Youth, 1964), p. 10.

harassment, peremptory treatment, and disregard for the client's procedural rights and the formally prescribed standards of benefits. When the welfare worker's instructions to keep costs low, and the recipient's desire to increase his family's allotment conflict, as they often do, the worker usually prevails [2] —despite the supposed availability of hearing procedures designed to protect the welfare client against unlawful, arbitrary, or unreasonable decisions.

From January 1964 to February 1967 MFY's Legal Unit handled more than five hundred cases in welfare law, which amounted to 13 percent of the total case load. The dramatic increase in welfare cases in 1966 and 1967 can be attributed partly to the activities of welfare recipients' organizations and partly to the neighborhood's growing familiarity with the Legal Unit. Approximately 85 percent of the welfare cases originated in arbitrary, unreasonable, or illegal decisions of the welfare worker. The unit developed a variety of tactics to handle such cases. In addition it challenged a number of Department of Welfare policies which acted to limit the clients' exercise of their rights. This paper describes those tactics and challenges.

The Weapon of the Fair Hearing

In 1961, the New York Department of Welfare received more than 250,000 applications for assistance, of which 39 percent were rejected. Despite the fact that fair hearings on rejected appeals must be held if requested by an applicant, few of these rulings on eligibility were challenged. In New York, fair hearings are administered by the New York State Department of Social Welfare, and the hearings are held before a referee supplied by that department. The fair hearing is a means by which the State Department of Welfare can fulfill its function of policing local welfare agencies; the state is responsible for investigating a complaint and is em-

[2] For a complete description of the origin of these problems see the chapter on "Organizations of Welfare Clients" in Vol. 2, *Community Development.*

powered to reverse local decisions which violate state or Federal regulations.

Typically the state will pressure a local department to settle a case involving flagrant violation of welfare laws. This pressure is in the form of an investigation made by the state for each fair-hearing request, which often includes interviews with both the client and the welfare staff, plus a review of the local department's files. The state's intervention can prove very embarrassing to a local department that is clearly in the wrong. Consequently, few hearings actually take place, for the local agencies reverse their rulings rather than risk an adverse state ruling or a state investigation. Only when the local agency is confident of winning its case will a fair hearing be held.

Federal regulations require fair hearings to be held within sixty days of the request. Written arguments (briefs) are presented by each party (the welfare client or his representative and the Welfare Department), and decisions must be handed down by the state referee within thirty days. Local welfare agencies have another thirty days in which to implement the ruling. Thus a welfare client may be forced to endure illegal deprivation for four months. In fact, in several cases it has taken six months before the hearing process was completed. The length of time it takes to reverse a decision remains a major defect of the fair hearing and detracts from its usefulness as a remedy for the welfare recipient.[3]

[3] For this reason Legal Unit attorneys are more frequently seeking a court order of mandamus, which requires public agencies to perform their legal duties and conform to legislative requirements. Mandamus orders are sought in the State Supreme Court and usually receive judicial consideration within twenty-four hours of application. The court orders are binding upon the state agency and have precedent value when written opinions are obtained. Mandamus requires a ruling on the central question of whether the practice at issue is in conformity with the law; it does not apply to cases in which the law itself is challenged. The value of an order of mandamus lies not only in its speed but also in the fact that it extends judicial scrutiny into areas of public administration which have received little review by the courts. The Legal Unit in 1967 took an action in the U. S. District Court of the Southern District of New York which would mandate the Welfare Department to hold a fair hearing before a client is suspended. The action is still pending decision. In the meantime the state Welfare Department altered

Fair-hearing procedures and the mandamus process to challenge welfare decisions were virtually unknown when the Legal Unit began its work. The right to appeal was not publicized, and few recipients had prior knowledge of it. The welfare client who had no knowledge of the rules and procedures was unlikely to set about appealing the decisions of a caseworker without the aid of an informed professional.[4] In addition, there is no provision for legal representation of a client at the fair hearing. Therefore the few clients who had the knowledge, courage, and persistence to carry through a fair-hearing request were placed in an obviously disadvantageous position: They had to present and defend their cases unassisted against the attorneys of the Department of Welfare. There was, in effect, no means of enforcing the right to appeal.

MFY's neighborhood service centers and the welfare-recipient organizations are the sources of welfare-case referrals for the Legal Unit. When a welfare problem is brought to a center, a neighborhood-service-center worker first negotiates with the Welfare Department in the client's behalf. If results are not forthcoming, the client is referred to the Legal Unit. Unit lawyers are less willing to spend time negotiating with a welfare worker, since this has proved fruitless and prolongs the client's deprived state; usually a fair-hearing request is filed immediately. In the estimated 20 percent of cases which involve negotiation in advance of a hearing request, the intent is to inform the welfare worker of the law and persuade him of the legality of the client's position. The threat of litigation is often enough to bring about resolution of the problem.

Yet by mid-1967 more than three hundred fair-hearing requests had been filed by the Legal Unit. An estimated 95 percent of these

its policy; it now requires a conference between worker and client before a suspension is brought, arguing therefore that the court should not hear the case since the difficulty it seeks to rectify no longer exists.

4 There is evidence that it was the policy of the New York City Department of Welfare to withhold information about the right of appeal from its clients. The former director of the unit recalls that in drawing up the appeals on the Welfare Abuse Law, he requested a copy of the regulations pertaining to the fair-hearing process. At first he received no answer; after repeated requests he received a partial copy of the rules. Finally he had a full copy smuggled out of the Welfare Department.

were settled in favor of the client before the fair hearing was held. Another 4 percent of the cases were dropped before the hearing because of changes in the client's circumstances. In addition to securing legal entitlements for clients, fair hearings were used to challenge a variety of policies of the Welfare Department.

Applications of the Welfare-Abuse Law

The Welfare Abuse Act of New York is based on the old myth that the poor move in search of the most generous welfare benefits. In 1960, when large numbers of southern Negroes and Puerto Ricans were coming to New York City, after an intense public controversy, a bill restricting welfare eligibility to New York residents was passed by the state legislature and vetoed by Governor Rockefeller. Had the bill passed, in-migrants would have had to wait at least one year before they could receive aid.

The following year, against the opposition of the governor and of state and city welfare agencies, a compromise bill was passed. The Welfare Abuse Act did not require a welfare applicant to be a state resident in order to be eligible, but the applicant had to show that he had not come to New York "for purpose of receiving such public assistance and/or care." Emergency aid was to be provided to all applicants regardless of their motivation in coming to New York. The public had confidence that few, if any, applicants would be barred from some kind of assistance by this new welfare law.

It soon became apparent, however, that the law was being applied more strictly than anticipated. In the first ten months of its operation, 2,730 applicants were ruled ineligible, and 387 of these had also been denied emergency assistance as provided by the law. By the time the MFY Legal Unit began its functioning, rejection of welfare applicants on the basis of the Welfare Abuse Law was so serious that it became the focus of the unit's first test case in welfare law. The administration of the Welfare Abuse Law had become one of the major problems facing MFY clients. The legal and moral issues were clearly defined, and the concerted efforts of

MFY social workers had failed; there was no alternative but to initiate a test.

An analysis of the law's administration made it apparent that most applicants were being disqualified or denied emergency aid on the basis of two presumptions:

> (1) that a person who comes to New York without an adequate plan of support, and possibly knowing that he will need welfare help, *therefore* comes for the *purpose* of obtaining welfare help;
>
> (2) that emergency aid under the Welfare Abuse Act should be given only to those who agree to leave the state.

The poor move for a variety of reasons—in search of work, to be near relatives, to better their way of life, etc. Most of the poor are unskilled, most are poorly educated, and few are well informed about the new environment they will find. It is unreasonable to demand that such people formulate a plan of support in advance of their arrival. While most in-migrants come with some notion of what they intend to do, their lack of information and experience in the city clearly preclude exact planning. Furthermore, the first presumption conflicts with the consensus among social workers, urban historians, and students of migration patterns, that it is the search for better social and economic opportunities that underlies the movement to the city.

The second assumption—that emergency aid should be granted only if the applicant agrees to return to his home state—is against the Welfare Abuse Law itself and the Department of Welfare procedural regulation, which specify no limit on eligibility for emergency assistance. Such a practice raised other, more fundamental issues. For example, pressure on an applicant to leave the state combined with a one-year residency requirement constitutes a state-enforced restriction of freedom of movement.

After extensive interviews with MFY social workers and welfare clients, the unit selected several cases for appeal, each involving a clear-cut violation of the intent of the law and serious deprivations for the families concerned. Among the cases were the following:

A young man had become a drug addict soon after marriage. His mother sent the young couple to St. Louis to escape the drug environment, but within a year he was back on drugs. The mother then had the couple and their two children return to live with her so she could try to combat the drug problem. The family was denied assistance and was offered return transportation to St. Louis.

A young woman with a two-month-old child and a five-year-old godchild had come to New York to live with her grandparents, who were her only relatives. The Welfare Department refused to grant emergency assistance unless she left her children with the grandmother, a fragile, senile woman, and sought work. When she refused, she was rejected for any kind of assistance.

A young mother came to New York with her six children in search of her husband, who had preceded her, and also to be with her parents. When she first arrived, she was able to stay with a cousin in a public-housing apartment. Because of the size of her family, they had to leave public housing and were forced to live in tenement hallways. When the family came to the attention of MFY, it was on the verge of starvation, living in a dank basement without lights or toilet facilities. The mother and six children had been repeatedly denied emergency assistance on the basis of the Welfare Abuse Act.

Several of the cases were settled by the Department of Welfare in advance of a fair hearing. In the third case above, a state fair-hearing referee explicitly rejected the city's presumption that Señora R. had come to New York to receive public assistance. The state argued that even though "the appellant may not have had a reasonable plan to support herself and her children, and may even have realized prior to coming to New York that she might need public assistance," her motivation for coming to New York was to be with her parents, not to obtain public assistance. The state decision was also critical of the Department of Welfare for not properly administering the emergency-aid provision of the law, which was intended to benefit all newcomers, regardless of their purpose in coming to New York.

The state decision was not enough to eliminate improper applications of the Welfare Abuse Act. In the fall of 1964, approximately a hundred cases were appealed before the Department of Welfare formulated a set of guidelines for the administration of emergency aid. These new regulations have largely eliminated the problem of eligibility connected with refusals to return to another state or with issues of motivation in coming to New York. The new policy contains the following important points:

> No rejection at intake because of Section 139a; emergency aid to be granted at intake or during investigations where need is indicated; where Section 139a is applicable, emergency aid and return transportation will be offered and aid is to continue as long as needed; regular assistance to be given even if Section 139a is applicable in cases where it is judged in the client's best interest not to return to point of origin; after one year client will have gained residency even if Section 139a was applicable.

The effect of the legal action was not to challenge the law itself but to attack the presumptions upon which the law was being applied.[5] Although the challenge, ruling, and policy change all took place within a system of welfare appeals, the importance of legal representation is clear. The legal contribution in this case was to establish the entitlement and to facilitate the humane policy which had been urged from the first by the administrator of the New York Department of Welfare.

Psychiatric-Commitment Procedure

In the spring and summer of 1966, the Legal Unit represented several welfare clients who had been involuntarily committed by the Welfare Department to Bellevue Hospital for psychiatric observation. In each case it appeared that the welfare recipient had been committed without proper examination beforehand and apparently in retaliation for "troublemaking." When the cases were

[5] The U. S. Supreme Court will be deciding in 1969 on the constitutionality of welfare-residency laws. Three lower courts have already declared them unconstitutional.

brought to the attention of the Welfare Department, they were dismissed as isolated incidents. However, during the summer, several more clients were represented in commitment proceedings, and a group of similar cases was described to the unit by an attorney in the Harlem office of the Legal Aid Society.

Involuntary psychiatric commitment of welfare recipients by the Welfare Department generally followed a troubled and difficult relationship between client and caseworker. The client usually received no notice of the visit by the welfare psychiatrist or the intended examination. The welfare psychiatrist did not identify himself as such, or was falsely identified at the home visit. The psychiatric examination itself was brief, cursory, and inadequate, the doctor relying almost totally on the caseworker's reports. In almost every instance, the grounds for commitment were subsequently contradicted after a more thorough examination by hospital or independent psychiatrists. Finally, the welfare psychiatric examination was often related to Welfare Department-initiated child-neglect proceedings—that is, the recipient's commitment was the occasion to obtain custody of the children.

In August 1966, the Legal Unit sent the commissioner of welfare a detailed presentation of the problem, including illustrative cases, a definition of the pattern in the cases, and proposals to remedy the situation. In that same month the Legal Unit was contacted by the director of psychiatry of the Department of Welfare. At a meeting in October, the director of psychiatric services made the following points:

1. A reorganization of the Department of Welfare's psychiatric procedures was under way.
2. The psychiatric services were performed by psychiatrists selected from panels attached to each welfare center and paid per visit. It was the director's opinion that these psychiatrists were probably incompetent and incapable of surviving in private practice. He expected that payment by the visit minimized the time spent in each analytic interview.
3. The panels were to be replaced by consulting psychiatrists, paid

on a monthly basis and responsible for approving all psychiatric visits, interpreting client behavior to caseworkers, and mediating worker-client conflicts. Such mediation might eliminate the need for 80–95 percent of the home visits made currently.

4. All psychiatric problems with clients were to be taken up with the consulting psychiatrist; possible action was to be a joint decision of the consultant, a medical social worker, and the welfare worker. Consideration was to be given to preparing the client for the visit.

The unit proposed that the department give the recipient written notice of the time, place, and purpose of the visit, and that they recognize the client's right to be examined by a psychiatrist of his own choosing. The Welfare Department agreed to give prior notice and pointed out that the choice of an alternate doctor was made possible by the state Medicaid Program. There was disagreement over whether a client could be compelled to submit to an interview or go to Bellevue for observation. Unit attorneys stressed the vulnerability in the event of personal conflict with the caseworker and asked how the client was to be protected against false or malicious reports by a vengeful investigator. These issues were left unsolved and therefore unchanged.

The new psychiatric procedures met unit demands in the following ways:

1. The economic incentive underlying short interviews and inadequate analysis was eliminated.

2. Approval of a psychiatrist was required before an interview could be scheduled.

3. Psychiatrists would help with difficult worker-client relationships by interpreting the client's behavior to the welfare worker and thus increasing the worker's understanding of the case.

4. Clients were to be given prior notice of a psychiatric visit, and clients were to be allowed to choose their own doctor.

5. The new procedures provided institutional safeguards against the arbitrary use of psychiatric commitment proceedings as a weapon against uncooperative clients.

Since these points have been implemented, not one case of improper psychiatric commitment of a welfare client has been brought to the unit's attention. The Legal Unit in this instance provided a welfare program director with support for his efforts at improvement.[6] The unit's intervention probably ensured the prompt implementation of a revised procedure, more protective of the welfare recipient and oriented toward the client's legal rights. Unit lawyers, sensitive to arbitrary or unfair treatment of the welfare client, raised procedural points—prior notice, free choice of the examining doctor by the client—which might otherwise have been overlooked by the best intentioned nonlegal decision maker.

The Right to a Telephone

A good illustration of illegal arbitrary policies which evolve unchallenged in the administration of public welfare was the practice of denying the welfare recipient the right to a telephone. The telephone policy was based on Section 215 of Policies Governing the Administration of Public Assistance, which prohibits welfare recipients from having telephones without demonstrated medical, employment, or social reasons.

In some cases, the discovery of a phone in a recipient's home led to termination of benefits. The enforcement of the policy often involved serious invasions of recipient's privacy. Caseworkers frequently would arrive unannounced, make an intensive search of the client's house, and utilize various subterfuges to expose a concealed phone. Recipients often told of keeping their telephone secreted in closets or under the floor, fearful that the phone might ring during a welfare worker's visit!

As with other policies, enforcement of the telephone ban was determined by the individual welfare worker. Some caseworkers took a permissive attitude toward telephones and would support a client's request for one; others constantly ferreted out unauthorized phones and used the discovery of a telephone as ground for discontinuing all assistance. The worst effects of the policy can be spelled out in terms of human isolation: aged parents cut off from

[6] Then-Commissioner of Welfare Ginsberg was also quite eager that the situation be remedied, once it was brought to his attention by the Legal Unit.

their children, mothers and children cut off from community services or fire and police protection, the loneliness of those who for various reasons are seldom able to leave their apartments.

A unit attorney took up the issue on behalf of Mrs. P. who was threatened with loss of Aid For Dependent Children benefits for the unauthorized possession of a phone. A fair-hearing request was filed and an initial hearing held. The unit simply pointed out that the Social Security Act requires that AFDC benefits be extended in the form of money payments, and that according to the Federal Handbook of Public Assistance Administration, the money is to be spent as the welfare recipient wishes, without interference from the welfare agency. The handbook states this explicitly:

> Payment must be accomplished without direction on the check or by letter, or by agreement as a condition of receiving the payment, or by other notification, that the recipient must use his money in a specified way or for a specified purpose.

The Department of Welfare abandoned its defense in the case before a fair hearing was held and issued a statement of revised policy in July 1966. The statement read in part:

> . . . the family has the right of self-determination as to how this grant should be spent. As long as the family's expenditures do not involve the provision of additional funds by the Department, there should be no restriction as to the use of the funds granted. . . . This therefore applies to the family's decision to have a telephone.

In the MFY area the right to a phone is no longer a problem; whether the revised policy is being observed in areas where militant advocacy of welfare recipients' legal rights does not exist is an open question.

Since the revised policy went into effect, the issue has shifted from the client's right to have a phone to the right to a phone where the Department of Welfare must provide funds for it. A client may receive a special grant for a telephone when such service is essential to health and safety, producing an income, or maintaining contact with community agencies, relatives, or persons essential for service.

Throughout the fall and spring of 1966 the Local Unit conducted a campaign to obtain telephones for welfare clients. As of March 1967, eighty-six clients had sought the assistance of the Legal Unit, forty-three of whom were clearly ineligible for a special telephone grant. Of the forty-three who were eligible, fourteen had obtained phones, three grants were denied, and twenty-six were in the process of obtaining a fair hearing. The ineligible clients were those who did not have a serious medical problem or strong social justification—large numbers of children, etc.—for a phone. When a client did not meet the legislative standards, there was little that could be done.

Minimum Standards

In November 1966, after a year of activity by welfare organizations and the Legal Unit, the Department of Welfare revised its minimum-standards policy.[7] Where previously the department did not accept the responsibility of informing the client of what he was entitled to by Federal and state law, the department now accepts the responsibility for *initiating* an assessment of the client's needs in winter clothing and household effects. Department Informational No. 66–48 states simply:

> The Department is committed to the principle that clients should be brought up to minimum standards, as defined in the manual. If this was not done when the client's case was opened, the client's needs in relation to minimum standards should be discussed *on the initiative* of the worker during statutory visits. Achieving minimum standards should be a regular part of accepting a new case for public assistance.

[7] For an analysis of the part lawyers played in the minimum standards campaign see the chapter on "Organizations of Welfare Clients" in Vol. 2, *Community Development.*

Although the clarification of minimum-standards policy was a response to the continued pressure of the welfare recipients' organizations, the Legal Unit attorneys played an important role in formulating strategy, drawing up appeals, and writing letters of support. Demonstrations and mass requests to be brought up to standard in conjunction with the use of legal forms of pressure (fair-hearing requests) have resulted in a clear liberalization of the administration of minimum standards.

Procedural Rights

Cases represented by the Legal Unit have also effected changes in the procedural rights accorded to clients by the Department of Welfare. The two most important instances of change involve the establishment of the right to have a third person participate in welfare interviews, and the right of a client or his representatives to consult Welfare Department records in advance of a fair hearing. These cases have contributed to the growth of due process of law in the administration of welfare.

In the case of Mrs. S., summarized below, the Legal Unit won the declaration of a welfare client's right to third-party assistance in dealings with the Welfare Department.

Mrs. S. is fifty-eight years old and does not speak or understand English. At the time she came to MFY for assistance she was living with her daughter, two grandchildren, and one great grandchild. The family was existing on fifty dollars a week earned by a granddaughter and was in dire economic straits. Mrs. S. sought the assistance of MFY in applying for public welfare. Subsequently, the department refused to accept or process an application in the presence of the MFY worker who had accompanied Mrs. S.

After negotiations with the department failed to produce results and an intervention by the State Department of Welfare was inconclusive, unit attorneys prepared a mandamus petition to the New York Supreme Court, asking the court to direct the commissioner of welfare to fulfill his legal responsibility by processing the

application. Although the Department of Welfare was now prepared to accept Mrs. S.'s application, the Legal Unit was determined
to carry through the mandamus proceeding unless the department
agreed to spell out a change in policy. Under the threat of court
action, the department drew up a memorandum accepting the
principle of third-party help. In January 1967, the Department of
Welfare issued an informational policy statement which confirmed
the client's right to third-party assistance. The passage of relevance
is as follows:

> An applicant for, or recipient of, public assistance has the right
> to have another person with him at the time of his application for
> assistance in the Welfare Center or at other contacts or in his home.
> The presence of a third person . . . is permitted as long as it is the
> desire of the applicant or recipient . . . and . . . shall in no way
> affect the determination of initial or continuing eligibility, nor shall
> it affect the processing for care or service.

This change was instituted because the unit insisted on an overall
policy change rather than accept an immediate settlement of Mrs.
S.'s problems.

The establishment of the second change in procedural rights—
the right to consult Welfare Department records in advance of a
fair hearing—was effected by the case of A.R. Several times during the preparation of the brief, unit attorneys asked to see the
department's case records. The requests were never acknowledged.
The unit subsequently brought a mandamus proceeding to secure
the procedural rights of fair hearing as set forth in the Federal
Handbook of Public Assistance. At issue was the "Federal requirement that state fair-hearing proceedings allow the appellant an
opportunity to examine written evidence prior to the hearing."
This right had been repeatedly denied, in violation of the statutory
requirement that state regulations conform to Federal regulations.

Prior to the hearing, the New York State Department of Welfare
agreed to revise its rules in accordance with the Federal requirements. State fair-hearing regulations were amended to establish
a procedure by which the attorney of a welfare client could obtain

copies of all documents to be introduced by the local welfare department in the fair hearing. The definition of this right, with its implications for the justice of the appeal process itself, is perhaps one of the Legal Unit's most important contributions to the administration of welfare law.

Conclusions

The influence of the Legal Unit upon the interaction of the Department of Welfare and its clientele can be measured in several ways: in terms of substantive changes in welfare law, in the form of administrative procedures or policies, and in terms of services and benefits provided to the welfare recipient, such as assertion of procedural rights, prevention and control of unwarranted invasion of privacy or harassment, and enforcement of state and Federal minimum standards.

The continuing presence of legal advocates affords assurance that other discriminatory practices will not evolve in the future. In the past, illegal administrative practices have flourished unhindered because the clients did not know their rights, court precedents were lacking for welfare decisions, and the appeal process itself was largely unused. Legal representation exerted pressure on Welfare Departments to formulate more specific procedural guidelines for their workers.

This point brings into focus two important nonlegal results of legal advocacy of the rights of welfare clients: the attempt to equalize the worker-client relationship, and the activation of the welfare appeals system.

The unequal nature of the worker-client relationship derives from the discretionary power of the worker regarding benefits and the client's lack of knowledge of his rights, sources of help, and confidence to assert them. One of the major contributions of the Legal Unit in providing representation to welfare clients has been to make the client less vulnerable.

In cases where a client's assertion of his rights has led to threat and harassment, the intervention of an attorney has put an im-

mediate end to such problems. More important, the very existence
of such support has made the welfare clients themselves more willing to pursue their legal benefits and assert their procedural rights.
By protecting the client against retribution by vindictive workers
and supervisors, the Legal Unit has helped to create a climate in
which clients feel that they can assert their interests effectively.[8]

The unit's activities also tended to make welfare workers more
accountable for their decisions. Workers became more cautious
about decisions against the client when arbitrary or unfair rulings
risked being challenged in a fair hearing or subjected to judicial
scrutiny in a mandamus proceeding.

The development of the fair-hearing weapon has probably been
the most striking achievement of the Legal Unit in the field of
welfare law. After the pioneering work of the unit, the use of the
fair-hearing appeal has now become widespread in the New York
area. The complementary use of mandamus proceedings to ensure
that the Department of Welfare abides by its legal requirements
provided another basic tool for action in welfare law. These legal
remedies, in conjunction with the work of welfare-recipient organizations whose growth and development were assisted and sustained by the Legal Unit, had profound effect on the Department
of Welfare.

Mobilization's Legal Unit forced the Department of Welfare to
rethink policies and procedures which had developed unchallenged
over two decades—policies based on paternalism, on disrespect
and distrust of clients. The introduction of the process of challenge
on behalf of those whom the department is mandated to serve was
the central achievement of the Legal Unit.

The unit, as well as other MFY divisions concerned with welfare,
took the position that clients were entitled to the rights granted to
them by law. Although MFY efforts clearly provided clients with
effective tools for obtaining their rights, it is also clear that the

[8] Staff workers in the welfare organizations felt that, without assurances
from lawyers that they would protect clients' rights, many clients would be
too fearful to join such organizations.

system cannot operate effectively for the benefits of clients so long as holding down the cost of welfare remains the prime concern of those involved in its operation and so long as public indifference prevents a true confrontation with the basic causes of poverty.

7

Administrative Law: the Case for Reform

Michael Appleby and Harold H. Weissman

The poor, more than other segments of society, distrust and fear governmental agencies, because their encounters with these agencies are more likely to have crucial consequences for their future happiness and security. The work of the MFY Legal Unit clearly demonstrates that the administrative practices and policies which have grown up around these agencies are applied at times capriciously and at other times in ways that discriminate against the poor. This paper describes and analyzes the efforts of the Legal Unit to combat unjust practices in the public agencies concerned with housing and unemployment insurance as well as in the public schools.

Unemployment Insurance

The Lower East Side, like other poor communities, has more than its share of joblessness. At the time of the 1960 MFY survey, one third of the area's family heads were out of work; 12 percent had been without work for four to twelve months. High unemployment rates were reflected in dependency on state assistance programs. Forty-one percent of the families surveyed in 1960 received some form of public aid; 17 percent of family heads qualified for unemployment insurance benefits.[1]

[1] *A Proposal for the Prevention and Control of Delinquency by Expanding Opportunities* (New York, Mobilization For Youth, 1961), pp. 26–27.

Individuals who received unemployment insurance are the source of a small but significant portion of the Legal Unit's case load—between four and ten cases a month. With few exceptions, unemployment-insurance cases have at issue establishing an applicant's qualifications or affirming a recipient's continuing eligibility for benefits.

The New York Department of Labor, which is responsible for administering unemployment-insurance programs, exhibits a preoccupation, similar to that of the Department of Welfare, with the eligibility of its clientele. Yet there are considerable differences in the ways in which the two programs are administered. Disrespect for the client is much less pronounced in the administration of unemployment benefits. The procedures by which a client may appeal a ruling also differ in the two programs. In contrast to the Department of Welfare, the New York Department of Labor operates a well-articulated appeal system which gives an aggrieved client an opportunity to contest any ruling he feels to be unfair. The right of appeal is prominently described in the forms an applicant for unemployment insurance encounters.

The appeal involves first an appearance before a referee who is empowered to affirm or reverse the original determination. If the appellant fails to obtain satisfaction here, he can carry the appeal to the New York Unemployment Insurance Appeal Board. A final remedy potentially available is that of continuing the appeal in the New York courts. However, reversing a Department of Labor ruling becomes increasingly difficult at each successive stage of the appeal process, particularly when the case is subjected to judicial scrutiny. The courts are loath to overturn a particular administrative decision because to do so would be tantamount to performing an administrative function for the agency concerned. The courts do not feel they have the expertise to administer. Therefore they usually restrict themselves to the issue of whether the requirements of the law have been met and whether the decision of the agency is reasonable; they generally will not consider the process by which the decision was reached or whether the decision was a wise one. This greatly narrows the basis upon which a court appeal can be made.

At the lower level of the appeal process, a considerable number of problems exist around the definition of "willful misrepresentation." The minimum penalty for an infraction is disqualification for five weeks of benefits. Most misrepresentation cases originate in the form in which the applicant must explain the reason for leaving or losing his job. The space allowed for the answer is very limited and does not permit lengthy or detailed explanations. The client must explain why he is unemployed specifically and in semantically correct terms. The phrases "I was laid off," "I was discharged," "I was fired," "no work," etc., are taken to represent distinct situations and must be used correctly if an accusation of willful misrepresentation is to be avoided.

Typical of the cases which Mobilization handled was that of Consuela V., who left her job in a leather shop because she could not afford to pay the union fee of fifty dollars on her weekly salary of fifty-five dollars. The union would not let her work without payment of the total amount. On the advice of another unemployment-insurance client, Consuela answered the question "Why did you leave or lose your last job?" with "No work." The Department of Labor ruled that Consuela had forfeited her benefits for twenty working days because she had left her employer without good cause, and she had willfully made false statements to obtain benefits. On an appeal to the referee, the first charge was dropped, but the charge that she had "willfully made incorrect statements" was affirmed. The referee was upheld by the State Unemployment Insurance Appeal Board, which found no error in fact or in the referee's opinion.

This ruling was affirmed despite the fact that Consuela spoke no English and had to have another client assist her with the form. She received no instructions on the use of the form or on the proper terminology to use from Department of Labor personnel. No effort was made to ascertain what Consuela meant by "no work," and in an interview one week later she made no effort to conceal the reason for leaving her job. It is clear that the language barrier complicated her understanding of the proper answer. The fact that the union refused to allow her to continue working could easily be interpreted by her as meaning "no more work."

The requirement that a client be semantically precise in explaining his unemployment or risk forfeiting benefits for willful misrepresentation works a real hardship on Spanish-speaking clients. Some Department of Labor centers have 85 to 95 percent Puerto Rican clients. To date no translators have been provided in these centers. When Spanish-speaking clients need help, another client who speaks both Spanish and English is recruited to translate. The applicant is responsible for any mistakes his makeshift interpreter might make and is liable for every statement despite his inability to judge the accuracy of the answers made on his behalf.

This procedure is not calculated to protect the best interests of the client. The crowded unemployment office, the client's uncertainty as to what is expected from him, and the desire of the volunteer interpreter to conduct his own business, all create an environment in which a Spanish-speaking client finds it difficult to make himself understood. Under these conditions, applications are often improperly filled out, and mistakes which cost the client his eligibility are common. Translation problems recur day in and day out; large numbers of applications for unemployment benefits are improperly rejected because of language difficulties. Most of the unit's cases in this area, like the one described above, involved some sort of language difficulty.[2]

Another source of problems is the work book, in which the client is required to record his work for each day of the week. The difficulty originates in the absence of standards as to what amount of time should be recorded. For each day of the week there is a box in which the client is to enter "Y" or "N" for "yes" or "no," to indicate whether he worked on that day. There is no explanation of what a proper yes or no answer signifies. In the belief that one

[2] The Legal Unit sought permission from the New York Office of Unemployment Insurance to post signs in Spanish advising clients of the availability of legal assistance and to train Spanish interpreters. Neither request was granted. An MFY lawyer did translate a book of regulations into colloquial Spanish, which the office promised to distribute.

or two hours of work does not constitute a day's work, clients frequently will ignore them in the record for the day. The unemployment office, in turn, often checks a client's work record by writing to the employer. If it is discovered that several hours of work were not recorded the client is accused of willful misrepresentation. This problem could easily be averted by an explanation of work-day standards as well as the proper way to fill out the form.

Some clients are declared ineligible because of faulty communication between the agency and the employer. Generally, the unemployment office verifies a client's answers by telephoning the employer and sending him a form. Frequently the employer cannot remember who the client was or why he was discharged, or he may name one of several reasons the client was let go and inadvertently cause the client to be accused of willful misrepresentation. Sometimes a subordinate who had little to do with the client's work is contacted and ventures some incorrect reason for the discharge. In these and many other ways, incorrect information can plague a well-intentioned applicant. Wherever the client's story is at odds with the report of the employer, an accusation of willful misrepresentation is made. The client is thus extremely vulnerable to the will or whim of the employer, who is in a position to determine whether or not unemployment benefits can be obtained. This is a particularly serious problem for Negro and Puerto Rican clients who face discriminatory labor practices and are the most likely to incur the disapproval of their employers. It is not unusual for an employment case to originate in an employer-employee conflict; in such a case, the client is at a real disadvantage in presenting his side of the story.

In dealing with its unemployment-insurance cases the Legal Unit came to several conclusions concerning the unemployment-insurance appeal system. There was general agreement that the first-stage referees are neutral in their hearing of the cases; yet several important procedural flaws and political biases at the state level of the appeal system cast doubt on the equity of the procedure.

At the referee level it is doubtful that the hearing procedure allows the claimant's side of the story to be presented in full. In the first place, while other parties in the case (the Department of Labor and often the employer) generally have attorneys in attendance at each hearing, the claimant ordinarily does not have legal assistance in the presentation of his case. The disadvantageous position of a poorly educated, Spanish-speaking claimant in so unequal a situation is obvious. Rather than be allowed to tell his story in full, the claimant is often asked a series of questions which may fail to elicit the circumstances under which the loss of job occurred. The unemployment office also can take statements the client made at any time and use them against him at the hearings; the claimant is not informed of this possibility. A record of the hearing is not kept, and only the most general outline of the case is recorded. As a result, Legal Unit attorneys entering the case after the first hearing have no way of knowing what questions were asked and whether they were relevant. The attorney's position is very difficult if further appeal is to be pursued. Consequently, many referees, who repeatedly hear only the employer's or the unemployment office's side of the issue, come to accept the view that few claimants have justifiable complaints. It is probable that hundreds of questionable determinations by local employment offices are sustained under these conditions. If an attorney for the claimant were present, the outcome might be quite different.

A second major problem of the appeal system is its vulnerability to the influence of economic interest groups. The referees are civil-service appointees and are virtually immune to outside intervention. They are, however, affected by the State Appeal Board. The State Appeal Board is composed of political appointees, whose position and tenure are determined by the governor. Members of this board do not have civil-service protection and consequently can be subjected to political pressure.

The state government itself is responsive to the most articulate and organized pressure groups. In New York it is to the benefit of employers to keep down the number of their workers claiming unemployment insurance because the rate at which they must contribute to this program is inversely related to the number of such claimants. Thus the pressure on the State Appeal Board produces a bias against claimants and a general unresponsiveness to the needs of Spanish-speaking clients.

Referees soon learn what kinds of disposition are likely to be overruled and begin to avoid them when possible. Referees who make liberal decisions in favor of claimants will have them appealed by the attorneys for the State Department of Labor. An unfriendly State Appeal Board will reverse them, and further appeal, as noted, is possible but unlikely to get results. As a consequence, referees generally affirm the determination of the local unemployment offices unless they are clearly illegal. Hundreds of cases are heard daily, and most uphold the initial ruling.

Conclusions. Although the state undoubtedly is justified in checking on the eligibility of claimants for benefits, it must also see to it that the rights of clients are not abrogated. Without the work of the Legal Unit, scores of local residents would have been deprived of their earned benefits. Given the political orientation of the State Appeal Board and the reluctance of the courts to intervene in the procedures of government agencies, the potential for changing the administration of unemployment insurance through legal action seems limited.

Mobilization did make one significant and successful appeal. Marta M. was disqualified from receiving benefits on the ground that she had refused employment for which she was fitted by training and experience. Although Marta had six years' experience as a floor girl in a brassiere factory, she refused a similar job as a floor girl in a firm making housecoats. At the appeal before a referee, Marta explained that she had refused the job for reasons of health, but when she told this to a volunteer interpreter at the unemployment office (Mrs. M. neither speaks nor understands English), the interpreter advised her to offer the abbreviated explanation that the job was "not in her line of work." Marta further explained that she was allergic to wool, was under treatment for asthma, and had refused the job because she believed that it required the handling of wool. Her willingness to accept work was manifested by the fact that she accepted five other referrals and was subsequently hired at a corset factory.

Ignoring the language problem, the medical evidence, and Marta's willingness to accept other work, the referee sustained the initial determination, on the ground that Marta should have ascertained if she would actually have to handle wool. Thus, it was reasoned that she had refused employment without good cause. The decision of the referee and the local office was reversed by the State Unemployment Insurance Board, which accepted the medical evidence and Marta's clear willingness to take other jobs. The most important feature of the decision, however, was its treatment of the language problem. The point of interest here reads as follows:

> We find that there was a lack of communication between the unemployment office and the claimant, and there was also a question as to whether the volunteer interpreter adequately communicated the facts of the situation to the claimant.

The importance of this case, aside from the success of the appeal, lies in its potential as a precedent. Several appeals are pending at present which cite this finding.

Public Housing: Admission Procedures and Eligibility Criteria

Although cases involving public-housing tenants and applicants comprised only a small percentage of the unit's housing case load, they raised broad legal issues and are of special interest because they point to practices in the administration of public housing across the country.

Just as the New York State Unemployment Insurance system operates in a situation of conflicting interests, the New York City Housing Authority has its own special sets of constraints. The overriding factor which affects its work is the disparity between the number of families desiring public housing and the number of units available each year. According to estimates, 85,000 to 100,000 applications are received annually for the eight to ten thousand vacancies which open up in the same period.

The widespread demand for a limited supply of units has led to procedures which reduce to a minimum the consideration given to any application and to restrictive regulations which make tenancy insecure for some families. The disparity between demand and supply has also given rise to an attitude "on the part of those establishing standards for eviction from public housing in New York City that whatever rules they establish are merely a favor to tenants and the tenants have no right to fair standards of eviction." [3] The admission and eviction procedures of the Housing Authority are tangible expressions of such attitudes.

The activities of the MFY Legal Unit represent an effort to extend concepts of due process of law into public-housing administrative practice. The intent was to define tenant rights, and specify admission and eviction criteria and procedures as far as possible, so that areas in which the exercise of subjective judgment is required will be clearly recognized as subject to question, with the right of appeal guaranteed.

The local housing authority is required by Federal contract to make eligibility criteria public. [4] Despite this requirement, the Housing Authority considers these criteria a matter of internal administration and makes public only those relating to income and residence in substandard housing. Applicants generally have little idea of the numerous other factors that affect their chances of obtaining an apartment. Even efforts of the Legal Unit and other attorneys to obtain the criteria have, until recently, been obstructed by Housing Authority personnel, who have repeatedly denied the existence of any admission criteria which have not been made public. These additional criteria have come to light recently, however, and are central to this discussion.

The expressed objective of the admission policy of the New York City Housing Authority is "to create for its tenants an environment conducive to healthful living, family stability, sound family and community relations and proper upbringing of children." [5] The

[3] P. Kenneth Sprigs, "Eviction from Public Housing on the Basis of 'Nondesirability'," paper presented at the Seminar on the Indigent and the Law, New York University School of Law, Spring 1965.

[4] Public Housing Administration, Consolidated Annual Contributions Contract, Part I, Sec. 20, Admission Policies PHA 3010, October 1964, p. 8.

[5] Management Directive GM-1287, November 29, 1961.

Authority sets forth a policy designed to identify families which might obstruct the achievement of this goal by constituting . . .

. . . (1) a detriment to the health, safety or morals of neighbors or of the community; (2) an adverse influence upon a sound family and life . . . ; (3) a source of danger to the peaceful occupation of the other tenants; (4) a source of danger or a cause of damage to premises or property of the Authority; or (5) a nuisance.[6]

In arriving at such a determination Housing Authority officials are directed to consider . . .

. . . family composition, parental control over children, family stability, medical or other past history, reputation, conduct and behavior, criminal behavior if any, occupation of wage earners, and any other . . . information with respect to the family that has a bearing on its desirability, including conduct or behavior while residing in a project.[7]

Such standards are both broad and vague. Clearly the list of factors which could make a family ineligible is so extensive as to permit many abuses. More serious, however, is the fact that applicants are never notified of the standards being applied to them.

Information may be received from any source without verification, and the Authority's staff "during all preadmission contacts is to be on the alert with the applicant for any potential problems which were not previously uncovered." No provision is made for informing the applicant of adverse information, and the applicant does not know what information has been obtained and what will defeat his ap-

[6] Public and Community Relations Department, New York City Housing Authority, as quoted in Michael B. Rosen, "Tenants' Rights in Public Housing," *Housing for the Poor: Rights and Remedies* (New York University School of Law, Project on Social Welfare Law, 1967), p. 67; and from information supplied by Mr. Irving Weiss of the New York City Housing Authority on March 6, 1967, at a meeting between a committee of housing applicants, MFY legal staff, and representatives of the New York City Housing Authority.

[7] Resolution No. 62-9-683, Sec. 2, p. 1.

plication. There is no hearing on his application, and the applicant's only safeguard is the conscientiousness of the Authority's employees that the information will be carefully screened to determine reliability and relevance. But the safeguard is illusory, for the Authority has no evidentiary standards, and an applicant who has incurred the disapprobation of a landlord, neighbor, or social worker, or of Authority personnel with whom he has had contact, may be rejected without an opportunity to contest the determination.[8]

The grounds upon which ineligibility is determined include a record of arrests not followed by conviction, eviction from private housing for nonpayment of rent, irregular work history, a separation of husband and wife twice in the past five years, lack of furniture, grossly belligerent attitude in the application interview, four changes of residence within three years, and placement of a child with a relative or agency.

Many of these categories, such as those discriminating against broken families, have little basis in either state or Federal law, and yet have rarely been subjected to legal challenge. Rejected applicants have had little chance to contest this action because the criteria and the evidence supporting the rulings are, as noted, normally unavailable, the applicants may be timorous or uncertain of their rights, and legal counsel is absent. Aside from the inequities inherent in this situation, the actual procedures for processing applications present additional problems to the applicant.

For example, only those applicants assigned a high priority are investigated by the Social Consultation Unit. If these families, after investigation, are rejected, they are informed of the negative determination and are allowed, on request, to discuss the reasons at an interview. There is some doubt of the frequency or efficacy of such interviews.[9] Only those investigated by the Social Consultation Unit can request a meeting to discuss the reasons for a negative determination. But these families are relatively few. Thus a

[8] Rosen, *op. cit.*, p. 7.
[9] See Committee on Housing and Urban Development, Community Service Society of New York, "Memorandum on Housing Legislation, No. 4," January 26, 1967.

large number of applicants are declared ineligible without their knowledge and without an opportunity to explain their side of the evidence held against them. In addition, Legal Unit attorneys found many who, although eligible on the basis of income, state residency, and substandard housing conditions, had received no determination of eligibility or ineligibility in six- to ten-year waiting periods. Many such applicants continue to hope for admission to public housing long after they have been dropped from consideration. Others are mystified at seeing friends apply and be accepted while their own application goes unanswered.

Three of the Legal Unit's most important cases in public-housing law are related to admission procedures and eligibility standards. *Holmes v. New York City Housing Authority,* a group action taken on behalf of thirty-one applicants for public housing, attacks the legality of the admission procedure itself. The other two cases involve challenges by individual applicants to the specific criteria under which they were denied admission to public housing.

The Holmes case was the end product of a joint venture of the MFY Community Development program and the Legal Unit.[10] After the group of applicants had several planning sessions, a meeting was arranged for the presentation of their proposals to Housing Authority representatives. At the meeting, held on March 6, 1967, the applicants outlined their difficulties and pointed out several cases which illustrated the dimensions of the problem, among them an applicant who had waited thirteen years with no answer, a member of a job-training program who had been told he must have a job to be considered, a family with eleven children and no answer, and a welfare recipient ruled eligible but never admitted. Committee members also complained of an apparent bias against the admission of welfare recipients.

In response, the Housing Authority officials cited the extreme limitation of space and the large number of applicants. They categorically denied any systematic exclusion of welfare recipients. The

[10] See the chapter on "The Housing Programs, 1962 to 1967" in Vol. 2, *Community Development,* for a description of the organizational work upon which this case is based.

Authority representatives agreed to review the applications of each of the group members, to write personal letters to each explaining the status of his application, and to interview those whose applications were lacking some necessary information. However, they would not agree to notify other applicants of their eligibility or ineligibility, to make the admission regulations public, or to make any determination for applicants other than those for whom apartments were available. They argued that there was little point in processing applications when vacant apartments did not exist. Thus the committee was unable to win any broad changes in admission procedure.

When it was clear that satisfaction on the general procedural issues was not to be obtained by direct negotiation with the Housing Authority, a class suit challenging the legality of the admission procedures was instituted at the Federal district-court level. The court was petitioned to enjoin the New York City Housing Authority from continuing those procedures, on the ground that they "do not permit applicants to fairly compete for the few available apartments and therefore the plaintiffs are denied equal protection and due process of law. . . ." [11] According to the Holmes brief, the "deliberate discrimination" of New York City Housing Authority admission procedures . . .

> . . . means that those who are allegedly over-income or lack residence may immediately challenge the determination if they believe it to be in error, while those who are otherwise ineligible are not told and therefore cannot challenge the determination if they believe it to be in error.[12]

In the concluding paragraphs, the brief cites the cases of *Hornsby v. Allen,* dealing with denial of an application for a liquor license by the board of aldermen of Atlanta:

[11] *James Holmes* et al. *v. New York City Housing Authority,* United States District Court for the Southern District of New York, 1966 Civil Action File 2897, p. 2.
[12] *Ibid.,* p. 4.

The court . . . held that *"ascertainable* standards" had to be developed "such as order of application, which would determine in what order a benefit would be granted to equally qualified applicants." It would certainly be ironic if the court was more protective when applying for a liquor license than when applying for public housing, probably the only decent place to live available to the applicants.[13]

The importance of this case lies in the broad legal confrontation of the admission process. The issues raised by the Holmes case are fundamental; if the action is successful, it will lead to extensive change in the New York City Housing Authority application procedures. At this writing, the Holmes case is pending trial. In early 1968, the question of which court had jurisdiction over the case had not yet been decided.

A second important case involving admission to public housing is *Manigo v. New York City Housing Authority*.[14] The Legal Unit filed a mandamus proceeding to compel the admission to public housing of a family who . . .

. . . claimed that it was found ineligible on account of a prior record of the husband as a juvenile delinquent. The petitioner alleged that, although initially informed that her family would be admitted to tenancy, she was subsequently told "off the record" by Housing Authority personnel that because of her husband's record, involving three minor offenses at ages ten, fifteen, and eighteen, she would not receive an apartment although no formal denial of her application for admission would ever be made and her application would be allowed to expire.[15]

The Manigo case was important in that it was one of the rare instances in which the Housing Authority contested a mandamus proceeding and thereby risked judicial scrutiny of an eligibility standard and admission procedures. In previous cases, the Author-

---

[13] *Ibid.*, pp. 12–13.
[14] *Gilda Manigo v. New York City Housing Authority*, Brief of Petitioner-Appellant. Supreme Court of the State of New York No. 2197/66.
[15] *Welfare Law Bulletin*, No. 3, April 1966, p. 4.

ity had avoided a court test by admitting the applicant in question
(after some delay). More important, however, was the fact that, if
the claimant was successful, the Manigo case would not only provide the appellant with relief but would strike down this particular
eligibility standard and supply a basis for later legal challenges to
the New York City Housing Authority admission procedures. However, a decision was handed down against the Legal Unit in this
case by the State Supreme Court, and an appeal to the U. S. Supreme Court was denied certiorari.

Strawder v. New York City Housing Authority, a third case of
interest here, is less important for its legal impact than as an illustration of the typical course of a mandamus proceeding in behalf
of an applicant for public housing. Strawder had been rejected by
the Housing Authority on the ground that . . .

> . . . one of the applicant's children was having adjustment diffi-
> culties in school. Investigation by an attorney revealed the charge to
> be without foundation; school authorities gave the child an excellent
> report. It was suspected by counsel, however, that the real reason for
> rejection was the presence in the family of out-of-wedlock children
> who had been legitimized by the applicant's subsequent marriage to
> their father.[16]

A mandamus proceeding was instituted which claimed that the
eligibility standards and admission procedures of the Authority
violated the due-process and equal-protection requirements of the
Fourteenth Amendment. In order to avoid a test of its standards
and procedures, the Authority reversed its holding and agreed to
find the applicant eligible.

The Strawder case is representative of several cases in which
the Housing Authority avoided meeting the issue in court by reversing its original determination.[17] In such cases, when the ruling

[16] *Welfare Law Bulletin* No. 8, May 1967, p. 3.
[17] See Rosen, *op. cit.,* p. 35, note 21. In a recent case handled by MFY,
a mother living on a site about to be condemned was denied admission
because she had a "strange personality" and was "belligerent." Her bel-
ligerency consisted in refusing to accept substandard housing offered her by

of an applicant as ineligible is challenged by an attorney, the Authority will reinvestigate or sometimes hold a hearing for the applicant. The experience of the unit has been that the applicant usually receives an adverse decision in a hearing. The case is then taken to court under a mandamus proceeding, the Authority relents, a rehearing is held, and the applicant is found eligible. However, it should be noted that the scarcity of vacancies, the huge volume of applications, and the lack of the large apartments required by many low-income families narrow the base upon which successful challenges to improper determinations of ineligibility can be made. The unit experience is that, with few exceptions, only applicants who face serious emergencies can win admission to public housing. Applicants of lower priority, although equally eligible, are unlikely to obtain relief despite legal assistance.

Public Housing: Eviction Procedures

Another important aspect of the Legal Unit's experience with public-housing law relates to the eviction procedures employed by the Housing Authority. Although the protection of other tenants is clearly a legitimate function of the Housing Authority, the vagueness of some eviction criteria is conducive to arbitrary, unreasonable, or unconstitutional eviction proceedings. However, during the eviction process the tenant is given an opportunity to refute the charge of his undesirability in a hearing before members of the Housing Authority's Tenant Review Board. This hearing raises important due-process issues and is therefore the primary focus of unit activity in the representation of public-housing tenants.

The current procedure fails to meet the requirements of a fair hearing in the following specific ways:

1. *Notice.* The tenant receives such cursory notification of the eviction proceedings and the basis of charges that the preparation of a meaningful defense is precluded.

---

the Department of Welfare and in stating that she had a right to be admitted to public housing. When the Legal Unit informed the Housing Authority that it would bring suit to contest the Authority's determination, the Authority reexamined her application and found her eligible.

2. *Confrontation and cross-examination.* The sources of complaints and evidence against the tenant are not revealed. Hence the tenant is not able to question their veracity, to correct misstatements of fact, or to challenge the bias of complainants. The manager's dossier contains first- and secondhand reports of incidents, corroborated and uncorroborated, much of which would be rejected in a court setting as hearsay.

3. *Hearing record.* The right to the hearing is not established in the law; therefore the hearing is conducted informally, off the record. The absence of record limits the range of appeal to mandamus proceedings, which consider whether an action was arbitrary or capricious.

4. *Discovery.* Neither the tenant nor his attorney may consult the manager's dossier, which is the primary source of evidence for the hearing.

5. *Findings of fact.* There are no standards which determine what kinds of evidence may be considered and what kinds may not. As a consequence, a vast morass of detail is accumulated with little guidance as to the substantiation required.

Tenants have recourse to a further remedy: They may challenge the decision of the Tenant Review Board by instituting a mandamus proceeding. According to a unit attorney, there are three major bases for instituting such a proceeding in a public-housing eviction:

> One is that the whole procedure followed by the Tenant Review is improper, because it isn't a "fair hearing." The second is that the "facts" given by the Housing Authority as the basis for the eviction are untrue. And the third is that even if the facts are true, they do not constitute a justifiable reason for evicting the tenant.[18]

In contrast to cases attacking admission criteria and procedures of the New York City Housing Authority, by mid-1967 no cases involving the eviction of tenants have yet reached a court test, even though a number of tenant cases are still pending in mandamus

[18] Nancy LeBlanc, *Landlord-Tenant Handbook* (New York, Mobilization For Youth, 1965), p. 30.

proceedings. What is of interest here is the common pattern of litigation found in eviction cases. When a tenant is ruled ineligible at a Tenant Review Board hearing, the unit's practice is to institute a mandamus proceeding which challenges the final determination of the board on any or all of the grounds outlined above. The usual tactic of the Housing Authority here has been similar to that used in handling cases of applicants: The Authority refuses to meet the issues in court but simply petitions the court for a series of adjournments, sometimes over periods of several months and up to a year or more. After a series of adjournments, the Authority holds another hearing in which the tenant is reinstated and the eviction proceeding dropped. Most eviction cases handled by the unit followed this pattern. Other cases were settled at an earlier stage in the eviction process once the intervention of unit attorneys had become evident. To date, no tenant represented by the Legal Unit has suffered eviction from public housing. This fact reflects the unwillingness of the Housing Authority to subject its eviction criteria or procedures to judicial scrutiny.

Conclusions. Several conclusions can be drawn regarding the potential impact of legal representation of public-housing clients. Obviously, legal assistance provides the aggrieved applicant or tenant with a legal remedy for arbitrary, capricious, or inequitable treatment. This is particularly important with regard to evictions, where the standards are so vaguely defined, the procedures followed admit possible abuse, and the tenant appeal hearing has little relation to the original determination of nondesirability. On the other hand, it is clear that broad change in admission and eviction criteria and procedures is not likely to result from the unit's intervention in the near future. The response of the Authority to the intervention of the Legal Unit has been to delay the resolution of the case, to avoid a court confrontation, and finally to buy out the case by removing the original cause of the litigation. The Authority can protect legally questionable practices by reversing eviction proceedings or by admitting an applicant. The necessary procedural reforms therefore require legislative enactment. Such legislation will result only from the combined effect of legal and community political pressure.

School Cases

The most recent legal issues in public education have been concerned less with equality of educational opportunities than with the rights of individual students.[19] Legal challenges of school regulations or procedures have focused on three areas: regulations concerning marriage or pregnancy, dress regulations, and student rights in school-suspension hearings.[20] Since the New York City school system appears to be well ahead of the courts with regard to dress regulations, and cases involving exclusion from school for reasons of pregnancy have not been encountered,[21] suspensions are the primary source of Legal Unit school cases.

Poor neighborhoods contain many sources of school-behavior problems—broken homes, multiproblem families, alcoholism, mental illness, etc. It is not surprising that many children who come from seriously troubled families find it difficult to conduct themselves as required in school. On the other hand, school administrators who must deal with overcrowded classes, inadequate resources, high rates of turnover among teachers, and many other

[19] Harold Rothwax, Nancy LeBlanc, and William Resnick, in "Comment: The Rights of Public School Students," *Welfare Law Bulletin* No. 11, January 1968, p. 10, state: "Significant school issues, involving substantive freedoms, permissible regulations and penalties, procedures by which regulations are enforced, and the limitations of school authority have not . . . become great public or legal issues. They have received little attention despite the economic and social importance to the child of the decisions made by school authorities. Today, with a deepening appreciation of the demoralizing impact on the poor of many of our public institutional settings, and with the poor having new expectations in regard to official behavior, previously unnoticed issues are emerging."

[20] *Ibid.*, pp. 10–12, contains a full discussion of legal attacks on marriage and pregnancy regulations and dress regulations. For reports on school-suspension cases see *Welfare Law Bulletin* No. 9, p. 2, and No. 11, p. 9.

[21] *Ibid.*, No. 11, p. 11: "The Commissioner of Education of the State of New York, James E. Allen, ruled that New York schools do not have the right to ban merely unorthodox school attire [in that case the wearing of slacks]. . . . However, with regard to the exclusion from school for pregnancy, a Citizens' Committee for Children of New York study revealed that thousands of girls are suspended because they are pregnant. These cases have not resulted in legal action because the girls are not officially suspended, but instead are requested to voluntarily withdraw from school."

problems often find the disruptive student a serious threat to the precarious balance they have established among the satisfaction of the teaching staff, the maintenance of educational standards, and the orderly operation of the school. In this context suspension proceedings take on added significance. Although suspension from school may have severe consequences for the student's chance to obtain a minimum education, the suspension of disorderly students frequently appears to be essential for the efficient administration of a school. However, school authorities may be tempted to utilize the suspension prerogative before other alternatives have been exhausted. It is here that legal assistance can play a crucial role in the defense of a student's right to an education.

In school-suspension cases, as in the areas of public housing and unemployment insurance, there is a fundamental constraint upon the use of law as an instrument of change: The courts are unwilling to substitute their discretion for that of the administrative authorities.

> The general rule by which substantive regulations are tested is easily stated: the courts will not upset a school regulation unless it is arbitrary or unreasonable.[22]

Unless the attorney for the student can show a particular school regulation to be arbitrary or unreasonable, he must show that the behavior of the school authorities was inconsistent with the relevant regulation or legislative statute.

Although New York State law requires that any person between the ages of fifteen and twenty-one is entitled to attend the public schools where he lives,[23] a student may be suspended from attendance if he is insubordinate or disorderly, if his physical or mental condition endangers himself or other students, if he is too feeble-minded to benefit from instruction.[24] A minor who is sus-

[22] *Ibid.*, No. 11, p. 10.
[23] The Citizens' Committee for Children of New York, "Memorandum on School Suspensions," October 20, 1966, p. 1, quoting Sec. 3202 of the New York State Education Law.
[24] *Ibid.*, p. 2, quoting Sec. 3214 of the New York State Education Law.

pended as insubordinate or disorderly is to be immediately "sent elsewhere for instruction or steps taken for his confinement." With the written consent of the parent, a school may order a school delinquent to attend a special school or take other instruction under confinement.[25] A school delinquent is defined as a student who is "an habitual truant, or is irregular in attendance, or is insubordinate or disorderly during such attendance." [26]

The suspension procedure is officially described as therapeutic rather than punitive, and a student is to be considered for suspension only if, after "all available remedial procedures have been applied, a pupil remains disruptive or maladjusted to the extent that he does not profit from instruction or . . . prevents other pupils from learning. . . ." [27]

There are two forms of school suspension. A school principal can suspend a child for a period no longer than five days, after a presuspension conference "to try to resolve the problem at an early stage." If problems persist, a guidance conference is held to give parents, teachers, counselors, and supervisors an opportunity to plan educationally for the benefit of the child. Attorneys for the parent or the child may not participate in such a conference.[28]

If the problem requires more than five days to resolve, the case must be referred to the district superintendent for a guidance conference within ten days of the suspension. The principal must submit in advance of such a conference a report of the student's misbehavior in chronological order, and he must bring to the conference the pupil's official records, including health and test records. The parent must be notified of the conference, but if the

[25] *Ibid.* The consent provision here is illusory in the sense that a parent who fails to give his consent can be prosecuted in Family Court for violating a law which forbids inducing a child not to attend school. If the court fails to punish the parent, a "proceeding can be brought against the minor for violation of the compulsory education law."

[26] *Ibid.*

[27] General Circular No. 16, April 18, 1966, from the Executive Deputy Superintendent, as quoted in *ibid.,* p. 4.

[28] General Circular No. 16, as quoted in *ibid.,* p. 5.

parent fails to appear, the meeting can be conducted without him. It is this conference, at the district superintendent's level, that can have the most serious consequences for the student. The district superintendent must render a decision concerning the student within five days. The decision may involve . . .

. . . reinstatement, transfer to another school, referral for placement in a school for socially maladjusted children, referral to the Bureau of Child Guidance . . . for study and recommendation—including medical suspension, home instruction, exemption from instruction or referral to the Bureau of Attendance for court action.[29]

Once the child is suspended, his case must be "reviewed continually in an effort to explore every possible resource for the child." If necessary, the suspension will be continued until an available resource is located.[30]

This brief description of suspension is based on school regulations. There is, however, evidence that services for the suspended child are not available, that suspension proceedings are unfair to the child, and that, once a child has been suspended, his chances for future acceptance in school are adversely affected. The child's records are shared by school personnel participating in the conference; the case is discussed and the decision is made before the child and his parents are brought into the conference.[31] A study of school suspensions for 1965–66 found indications that . . .

. . . even the school personnel may be placed in a defensive position at such conferences. They feel they must produce story after story to make the child look bad, rather than suggest helpful measures. . . .

When the child and family are brought into the conference, they are treated in such a way that they must feel guilty and irresponsible, rather than be in a position to help solve the child's problems. . . .

[29] *Ibid.*
[30] *Ibid.*
[31] *Ibid.*, p. 7.

After this "conference" is over, the parent is told what plans have been made.[32]

At such conferences no one is present to help the child tell his side of the story or question those who have testified against him. "The theory says that the school is acting in order to help the child, so the child does not need help from anyone else." Further, although the regulations suggest regular review of suspension decisions and special school dispositions, "this does not seem to take place." [33]

The essential bias of suspension procedures against the student as well as the absence of objective consideration of his school needs is summarized by the Citizens' Committee for Children report as follows:

> In a sense, the suspension conference is used as an . . . administrative method to keep teachers happy by providing them with a sense of support. . . . There is a negative attitude toward permitting anything in the conference that might undermine the teacher in his attitude that suspension is there as an aid to him. Therefore, everything a teacher says in a suspension conference, or in the documents that go to the conference, is accepted as fact. The idea that a teacher might possibly be at fault or at least contributing to the youngster's behavior is ignored.[34]

The services which are supposed to follow a suspension were found to be generally lacking. In a sample of twenty suspensions, some students were found to have been suspended without services for one and a half to two years. Others had been suspended for six months as punishment for staying out of school for one year. When services were provided, they were found to be inadequate. The

---

[32] *Ibid.* ". . . in at least one district, the District Superintendent usually asks the child to tell the audience 'the bad things' he has done immediately upon his entering the conference. The same superintendent has been known to comment on the neatness or lack of neatness of the child during the hearing and involves the parent in his process of criticizing the child."

[33] *Ibid.*

[34] *Ibid.*, p. 8.

only resource available to many children was a 600 school for mal-adjusted children. Home instruction amounted to about one and a quarter hours a day on the average.[35] Finally, the Citizens' Committee for Children study found that information on many aspects of the suspension proceedings was not available. Many dimensions of the problem have yet to be uncovered.[36]

In general, the findings of the Citizens' Committee for Children of New York are consistent with the experience of both Mobilization For Youth social workers and attorneys of the Legal Unit. From 1962 to mid-1965, MFY social workers were allowed to attend district-superintendent suspension hearings. They found that the cases were discussed and decided before the child and his parents were allowed to come into the conference, that the conferences were generally held to ratify the initial suspension, that the child and his parent were given no opportunity to present their case or question the evidence against the child, and that the conferences regularly ignored the implications of the case for the teacher or the operation of the educational system. Furthermore, MFY social workers found the hearings to be considerably less therapeutic than the schools claimed. One MFY worker described the hearings in the following way:

> They seem to be a highly judgmental, moralistic, and debilitating experience, not only for the families involved, but for the school personnel as well. Since school personnel are placed in the position of being personally accountable for the child's difficulties, they

[35] *Ibid.*

[36] *Ibid.*, p. 9. According to the reply of the Bureau of Attendance to a Citizens' Committee for Children inquiry, information was unavailable on the duration of suspensions, the specific reasons for the suspensions, and the services available to suspend students. The Citizens' Committee for Children reports finding an informal suspension system, in which both school transfers and suspensions are conducted without reference to official procedures. No information on the numbers of students handled in this way was obtained. The Citizens' Committee for Children was also unable to obtain detailed firsthand information on what actually goes on in the conferences. In addition, there was no information on how many students, once suspended, were able to return to school. "Exactly what does happen, how much, and to whom, is not now known to us" (p. 10).

protect themselves by using page after page of anecdotal incidents about the child, which are used in the hearings often as an indictment and not in any sense in terms of understanding the family's position or in terms of seeing the way in which the school system fell short of meeting these children's needs.

For these children and their families, the hearing comes through as an awesome and frightening experience. To find oneself at the end of a long table, surrounded by strangers with "power," can be both confusing and upsetting. This, often combined with a language barrier, tends to make the families respond quite subserviently, and this subservience is reinforced by the structure and personalities involved in the hearings.

This social worker describes how some children were severely chastized for "impertinence"—any behavior which was not conforming. Such behavior as hyperactivity, name calling, and hitting other children was frequently described as "sick." The worker found herself interpreting aspects of low-income culture to the school authorities. Yet, she noted:

. . . each comment I make becomes applied to the individual case only, and there is absolutely no carry-over. . . . Thus the focus in the end gets turned back to the individual family's problem without looking at the way the current school structure may be demanding too much, may in fact be evoking acting-out behavior and [avoids looking at] its responsibility for working out alternative class structures, curriculum changes, etc.

MFY workers not only interpreted the ethnic and class culture with which the school authorities had to deal but followed up suspended students, looked into the backgrounds of the families involved, and talked to the teachers, principals, and guidance counselors concerned. However, in September 1965, as a result of increasing conflict with school authorities, the acceptance of MFY workers at suspension hearings was ended. It was at this point that the Legal Unit became actively involved with the issue.

In late 1965, the unit proposed to the superintendent of New York City schools that students should be provided with counsel at suspension hearings. The reply was that the hearings were therapeutic, not punitive, in nature, and that the provision of counsel was therefore inappropriate. A similar letter detailing the importance of counsel in hearings was sent to the chairman of the Board of Education of the City of New York, and once again elicited a reply in the negative. As a consequence, in May 1966, the unit initiated its first court action in a school-suspension case.

Major School-Suspension Cases: Cosme and Madera

Although there are a large number of suspension cases in which legal counsel might be of relevance, the cases actually brought to the MFY Legal Services Unit have averaged only two or three per month. In the spring of 1968, the unit litigated two school-suspension cases, *Cosme v. Board of Education* and *Madera v. Board of Education,* both involving the right of a student to have counsel present at a suspension hearing or guidance conference. The first of these cases is being heard in the state court system, the other in the Federal courts.

Tomasa Cosme had asked the unit for assistance for her son, who was in the process of being suspended from junior high school "on account of lewd, lascivious, and obscene language used to nearly every girl in his class. . . ." [37] Unit attorneys requested and were denied permission to attend the district superintendent's guidance conference. The unit then petitioned the Supreme Court of New York for a writ of mandamus to order the Board of Education to permit an attorney to attend the conference. The petition was dismissed on the ground that the conferences were . . .

. . . simply interviews or conferences which include school officials and the child's parents. Further, they are purely administrative in nature and are never punitive.

Respondent is not statutorily mandated to grant a parent a hear-

[37] Board of Education of the City of New York Answer, in Appellants Brief and Appendix, *Tomasa Cosme v. Board of Education of the City of New York,* p. A 22.

ing. Moreover, because the hearing or conference is administrative, the petitioner is not entitled to be represented by counsel.[38]

The court thus accepted the school's justification for the guidance conference and also the argument that the presence of counsel would turn the conference into a quasi-judicial proceeding rather than an educational discussion. Moreover, the court displayed the traditional reluctance to intervene in administrative matters:

> Respondent is vested with discretion in the performance of its duties. Only a clear abuse of such discretion is reviewable by a court, and no such unauthorized action here appears. Accordingly the petition is legally insufficient.[39]

Finally, the court argued that the administrative remedies within the school system (an appeal to the state commissioner of education for review of the case) were not exhausted and that therefore the court action was premature.

The unit appealed the decision to the Supreme Court of the State of New York Appellate Division, arguing that (1) principles of due process called for the right to counsel in school-suspension hearings, (2) it was not necessary to exhaust administrative remedies before bringing legal action, and (3) the hearings were in fact adversary and adjudicatory in nature. The Appellate Division affirmed the decision of the lower court without opinion.

The second important school case, *Madera v. Board of Education of the City of New York,* was brought into the Federal district court and may have far-reaching consequences. According to one review of the case, *Madera* is the first Federal case to "face squarely the problem of due process limitation on suspension hearings, and particularly on the requirement of right to counsel." [40] The unit is currently petitioning the Supreme Court of the United States for review of this case.

[38] *Ibid.,* p. A 2.
[39] *Ibid.,* pp. A 2–3.
[40] *Welfare Law Bulletin* No. 11, January 1968, p. 9.

The facts of the case are similar to those of *Cosme*. The parents do not speak English, their son had been accused of striking a teacher, and he was to answer a charge of juvenile delinquency in Family Court and, in addition, attend a guidance conference. Unit attorneys again had requested and been denied permission to attend the conference. They brought the case before the United States District Court for the Southern District of New York.

The decision reached is of interest. In the first place, the court held that, under the Federal civil-rights statute, it had jurisdiction over the case and that, contrary to the *Cosme* ruling, it was not necessary to exhaust all state administrative or judicial remedies before initiating legal action in a Federal court.[41] The court distinguished between the five-day suspension by a school principal and the longer suspension proceeding which involves the guidance conference at the district-superintendent level. The former proceeding is of little long-term consequence to the student whereas the district superintendent's guidance conference was seen by the court as involving very serious issues for the student. Perhaps the least of these was the loss of schooling for the student due to delays in obtaining appropriate program placement. The court found by reviewing school records that students were required to wait as long as six months before being admitted to a school for socially maladjusted pupils or as long as ten months before finding an institutional place.[42] Such delays can amount to expulsion from school or the loss of the student's right to attend school. Even more serious was the possible loss of liberty of either the child or his parents should the school raise the issue of neglect or delinquency in Family Court. Because of these potential consequences, the court found . . .

. . . that the due process clause of the Fourteenth Amendment to the Federal Constitution is applicable to a District Superintendent's guidance conference. More specifically, this court concludes that enforcement by the defendants of the "no attorneys" provision of

[41] *Madera v. Board of Education of the City of New York,* 35 U.S.L.W. 2620 S.D.N.Y. April 10, 1967.
[42] *Ibid.,* p. 22.

Circular No. 16 deprives plaintiffs of their right to a hearing in a state-initiated proceeding which puts in jeopardy the minor plaintiff's liberty and right to attend public schools.[43]

The court consequently enjoined enforcement of the "no attorneys" portion of General Circular No. 16.

The decision was appealed by the Board of Education, and in December 1967 a ruling setting aside the injunction was obtained from the Second Circuit Court of Appeals. In contrast to the lower court, which recognized the possibility that Family Court actions against the parent and child, or the functional equivalent of expulsion, might arise from the conference, the Circuit Court viewed the conference as a preliminary investigation which could result merely in a change of school assignment. For the appellate court the issue was "how the child may be returned to the educational system." It did not consider the more serious consequences of suspension, such as the long delay suspended students experience while awaiting assignment to another school or a more specialized institution, or the stigma attached to those placed in the 600 series schools for the socially maladjusted. As one observer states:

> The Circuit Court foresaw few serious consequences resulting from the conference, and viewed the hearing as an early step in necessary disciplinary procedures far removed from any delinquency adjudication.[44]

Moreover, the Circuit Court expressed the fear that the presence of a lawyer would transform the conference into a criminal adversarial proceeding.

> The conference is not a judicial or even a quasi-judicial hearing. Neither the child nor his parents are being accused. In saying that the provision against the presence of an attorney for the pupil in a District Superintendent's guidance conference "results in depriving plaintiffs of their constitutionally protected right to a hearing" . . .

[43] *Ibid.*, p. 23.
[44] *Welfare Law Bulletin* No. 11, January 1968, p. 9.

the trial court misconceives the function of the conference and the role of the participants therein . . . with respect to the education and welfare of the child. Law and order in the classroom should be the responsibility of our respective educational systems. The courts should not usurp this function and turn disciplinary problems, involving suspension, into criminal adversary proceedings—which they are definitely not. . . . The courts would do well to recognize this.[45]

The Circuit Court held that since the guidance conference is not a criminal proceeding, and statements of the conference are not used in any criminal proceedings, there is therefore no need for a counsel to protect the child's right against self-incrimination. On this basis, the court concluded that there was no constitutional command or any requirement of due process that authorized the presence of counsel at these conferences; it therefore removed the injunction of the lower court.

At the time of this writing, the unit is petitioning the Supreme Court of the United States for a writ of certiorari (review). But even if the Madera case is reviewed and a favorable decision is obtained, serious questions would remain. In the first place, there would still be no legal framework within the context of the guidance conference which would make the role of counsel meaningful. For example, who would compel the school authorities to allow the attorney to question those who have produced evidence against the child, or to examine the records on which the authorities base their decision? For that matter, who is to compel them to allow the attorney to present the student's side of the case? In the absence of such guidelines, the school authorities could in effect ignore the presence of an attorney. Unless the courts were to go beyond merely allowing counsel to be present at suspension hearings and define the role counsel might play in such proceedings, that role would remain at the discretion of the school authorities responsible for the hearings. Under such conditions, counsel for the student might be reduced to an ineffectual presence. The Madera case, if

[45] *Ibid.*, p. 9, quoting the text of the decision.

successful, is but one small step in a long process of defining students' rights in public schools.[46]

The Lawyer and Administrative Law

The following evaluation by Legal Unit Director Harold Rothwax, in particular reference to school cases, is also relevant to the experience of the Legal Unit in public housing and unemployment insurance as aspects of administrative law:

> Often the lawyer's tasks consist of presenting the reality behind the . . . humanitarian language with which administrative officials describe their institution. As the U. S. Supreme Court said in In re *Gault*, ". . . unbridled discretion, however benevolently motivated, is frequently a poor substitute for principle and procedure." . . .
>
> So few cases have been decided that . . . enumeration of what constitutes due process in many contexts of the school is impossible. It is incumbent on the lawyer to request, then demand, and, if refused, litigate to insure proper procedure . . . and put administrative authorities on notice that they are being observed.[47]

[46] Recently the unit has represented four suspended students who have experienced lengthy delays in being placed in an institution or being readmitted to school. The State Education Law (Sec. 3202) clearly states that all persons over five and under twenty-one years of age have a right to attend school. The unit has simply initiated a mandamus proceeding so that the student may claim this right. In each of the four cases, the student received an institutional or school assignment before the case came to court. In this way the problem of lengthy unserviced suspensions is being attacked. Thus far the schools have avoided a direct confrontation in court on this issue.

[47] Harold J. Rothwax, "The Rights of Public School Students," Conference Papers of the Ohio State Legal Services Association, 1968, pp. 204, 206.

8

The Law as an Instrument of Social Change *

Harold J. Rothwax

The Legal Unit has been successful in the individual cases it has handled; in general, those who have received the services provided have benefited greatly. Our success rate in terms of particular cases has been phenomenal. We have won or settled advantageously in more than 90 percent of our cases. This result, I think, suggests the need for this kind of legal service in the Mobilization area.

This kind of service, as distinguished from traditional Legal Aid services, is also important because Legal Aid, being remote, being centrally located, is not in a position to provide a continuing relationship with the people whose cases it handles. It has never been able to address itself to what we have come to believe are the most serious needs of poor people. We found very quickly, after opening up here, that the closest, most controlling, most continuous impingements upon the rights of the poor were by administrative agencies that had been set up to benefit the poor—public housing, the Welfare Department, boards of education, other agencies that were supposed to dispense and deliver the "new property," governmental benefits. Legal Aid had traditionally abstained from representing people in this area of administrative law, so that we provided a service which was never available before. Increasingly now, as a matter of fact, Legal Aid is responding to the needs of

* This paper is an edited transcript of an informal discussion with Harold Rothwax, director of MFY's Legal Unit.

the poor in administrative law and providing these services as well.

We were also able to add a different dimension to the services that had been provided. We attempted not only to do what Legal Aid had traditionally done—that is, wait until a person had an emergency and came seeking service, remove the nature of that emergency, and return that person to the community to await the development of a new emergency—but we also tried to treat the person in the context of his family and his community, treating not just the emergency he came in with, but all the subsidiary problems connected in one way or another with that particular crisis. If we found a person, for example, who was arrested on a criminal charge, we would represent him not merely in the case, but also on the issue of his housing if the Housing Authority moved to evict him as a result of that arrest. If he was suspended from his job, we might represent him before the employer who had refused to re-hire him. We would represent him in handling some of his debts which might have prompted his antisocial behavior in the first place. We tried to provide a comprehensive approach to the legal problems of a person, and through our closeness to the community and to the client we tried to develop a continuing relationship in the hope that the person through this relationship would come to know more about what his rights were, would feel freer about asserting those rights, and, most important, would come to us before the emergency arose.

Like the doctor, the lawyer is least able to be effective when an emergency has already arisen. All he can do then is try to mitigate the seriousness of the particular situation. To a large degree, we were successful in encouraging people to come in when they first begin to suspect that they had a problem with legal ramifications. The corollary of this emphasis is that we have tried to erase the defensive orientation which had been typical in the provision of legal services to poor people prior to the advent of neighborhood legal services. We tried to present legal services as a tool which the poor person can use aggressively to initiate action, not merely in responding to the action of others. In this sense, of

making the law an instrument at the service of the poor, I think we
have been very effective.

In the use of law as an instrument of social change, I think we
have been less successful. To put the idea of law as an instrument
of social change in some perspective, you have to realize that
before the advent of Office of Economic Opportunity funded
services a poor man was pretty much left to the kind of service
provided by a Legal Aid Society, an organization generally of long
standing, generally dependent upon private contributions, generally
paternalistic in stance and somewhat conservative in outlook, generally understaffed, overworked, and underpaid, and generally with
the attitude that providing these services was a type of charity and
not a matter of rights, an attitude that was not aggressive. Either
because of this attitude and approach or because of the circumstances under which they worked, the Legal Aid lawyer rarely
addressed himself to the substance of the law or the procedures by
which it was implemented. The Legal Aid Society, because it was
overworked and understaffed, was limited to the minimal role of
pulling the sting out of emergencies in the cases that were brought
to it.

A quick perusal of the laws that affect the poor and the procedures by which those laws are administered indicates that the
poor are at a disadvantage. The reasons are obvious. Law is not,
basically or primarily, a response to a sense of justice or injustice.
It is by and large a manifestation of power and the privileges and
preferences of those who have the ear of power. The poor have
not been heard, so the substance of the law does not reflect their
needs. In law school you take courses on creditors' rights, not on
debtors' rights; the reason is that creditors pay lawyers' fees.

When we first came into this area, we found out that there
were no cases in the whole area of welfare. The rules and regulations by which welfare operated were not even available. Similarly
in other agencies, the law, as it has been drawn up, has not reflected the needs of the poor. Even in agencies set up to help the
poor, the attitude of the bureaucracies has resulted in arbitrariness,
indifference, insensitivity, very often harshness and hostility toward

the intended beneficiaries. Whether this is the result of overwork, a remoteness from the ideals which originally inspired the legislation, or a generation of being unchallenged in the dispositions, the decisions, the administration of these programs is of little importance.

Obviously, if the Legal Unit program was going to succeed, some attention had to be paid to the substance of the law and the means by which that law was implemented. One of the problems we came up against was that, as long as we brought one case at a time challenging a widespread practice of long standing, the agency we were contending against could give us what that particular client wanted and buy us out, so that we could not persist and get a precedent-setting decision. That has been a real problem, although recently we have seen some erosion of this "mootness."

The problem, however, has led me to believe that one of the basic forces for social change in the law is a high case load. If the volume is very heavy, there is of course a distinct drawback in that it forces the lawyer to give less thorough attention to the details of each individual case, but a large case load has great advantages if it can be harnessed and used to effect change.

The fact is that, if the Welfare Department buys out an individual case, we are precluded from getting a principle of law changed, but if we give them one thousand cases to buy out, that law has been effectively changed whether or not the law as written is changed. The practice is changed; the administration is changed; the attitude to the client is changed. The value of a heavy case load is that it allows you to populate the legal process. It allows you to apply unremitting pressure on the agency you are dealing with. It creates a force that has to be dealt with, that has to be considered in terms of the decisions that are going to be made prospectively. It means that you are not somebody who will be gone tomorrow, not an isolated case, but a force in the community that will remain once this particular case has been decided.

As a result of this, in regard to the Welfare Departments, unheard-of things have happened. For example, we have been able, for the first time, to participate along with welfare recipients in hearings which affected the kinds of fair hearings that would thereafter be available to poor people. In other words, we participated in a rule-making process itself, in hearings that set the rules for fair hearings, a crucial point at which to safeguard the legal rights of the poor.

We have also, by virtue of our acquaintance with a great many cases, been able to see patterns emerge that would not otherwise be clearly noticed. One example is in the area of psychiatric commitments of welfare recipients. We were able, through handling a great number of welfare cases, to see certain abuses in the procedures by which recipients were committed to psychiatric observation—failure to give notice, failure to have a thorough medical examination, poor practices which allowed a psychiatrist to get paid more if he committed people than otherwise. Once we were able to see this pattern, we were able to bring it to the attention of the administrator and get the practice changed. Once it was stated, it was clear that the practice was an improper one. In terms of changing policy, by winning a great number of cases, in terms of being a force to be dealt with so that you can participate in the rule-making process (not just the decision-making process), in terms of being able to discern patterns as they emerge, law can, in a limited way, be an effective instrument of social change.

We have been less successful in court, in getting precedents and decisions which favor the poor, and in legislatures, in getting the passage of legislation of benefit to the poor. One reason for this, I think, is that the courts have certain traditions by which they interpret legislation. They are limited, of course, to determining whether or not legislation is constitutional or unconstitutional, and that is too gross a weapon, too severe a weapon, and one which the courts are traditionally reluctant to use. Apart from that, attitudinally, the judge is usually satisfied with the society that has recognized his merits sufficiently to elevate him to the bench. In his view, a society which has been that perceptive is generally not so bad. His role as a judge in society—the prestige and respect that attend that role—inevitably removes him from the area of the poor. He is either remote or, less frequently, hostile; in either event he is not able to sense fully what it is like to be poor and how the law bears upon the poor. Very often he brings the attitude of middle-class or upper-class society to his interpretation of a rule of law that is very far from the experience of the poor person.

There is also the limitation of the traditional role of the court in invalidating legislation. The courts, after all, are not a democratic agent in our society. By and large, either judges are appointed or they are elected in a process that rarely is concerned with their qualifications. Aware of this basically undemocratic system, the judges are therefore quite reluctant, often rightly so, to invalidate acts of elected legislators.

Another factor limiting the effectiveness of using test cases as an instrument of social change is delay within the courts. Our court system does not work well, especially when you have two large powers contending against each other. Insofar as legal services for the poor have become powerful, the agencies against which they contend have become more intransigent, and delay is inevitable. In one case, for example, in which we have been trying to get the standards regarding admission to public housing changed, the case has been in the courts for two years already, and we are still awaiting a decision as to the court's jurisdiction to hear the matter.

In most instances, our legal system breaks down under just the circumstances in which it is intended to operate best. Ironically, although we have an adversary system in which presumably, if both sides are represented, truth will emerge and the court will be able to reach the proper decision, in practice we find just the contrary. When General Motors contends against the United States of America in an antitrust case, the prospect is that it will go on for ten years with some kind of pyrrhic victory for one side or the other. Ultimately the parties realize that they are equal powers, apart from the justice or injustice of the position they maintain, and they come out with some kind of consent agreement about settlement which reflects not justice but the relative strength of the contending parties.

Our court system does not operate well when the parties have equal power because they both may persist for a virtually endless period of time. It works expeditiously when one party is powerful and the other is not, when the stronger can push the weaker party to some kind of clear result apart from whether it is a good result or a bad result. As legal services programs push for dramatic social change, they will engage the full resources of those they are contending against. These forces, with their power, will resort to all-out battles, to continual appeals which are going to delay clear-cut results. This leads to another point.

How clear-cut can a result be? What is the ultimate value of winning a test case? In many ways a result cannot be clear-cut. For example, this year, the United States Supreme Court is deciding upon the constitutionality of welfare residency laws, clearly a precedent-setting decision. But if the present welfare-residency laws are invalidated, it is quite possible that some other kind of welfare-residency law will spring up in their place. It is not very difficult to come up with a policy that is a little different, stated in different words, but which seeks to achieve the same basic objective. The results of test cases are not generally self-executing. I think this leads to the necessary conclusion that there is no law ultimately without lawyers to vindicate certain principles. It is not enough to have a law invalidated or a policy declared void if the agency in question can come up with some variant of that policy, not very different in substance but sufficiently different to remove it from the effects of the court order. You must have lawyers who can unremittingly attend to those variations, applying great pressure, using the power of the case load as the ultimate weapon that legal services for the poor possess. I don't think that the test-case approach can possibly succeed in achieving significant social change, and this has been the conclusion of most people who have worked with such an approach.

In any event, for all of the above reasons, I do not feel that we have been especially successful in getting wide, precedent-setting decisions to effect broad changes. We have been very successful in raising many issues and starting discussions and beginning the thinking process which may in the long run result in some change. But this is a long run we're talking about, it's gradual, it's far too slow; to my way of thinking, gradualism has always been the philosophy of the contented, the complacent, the people who are happy with the way things are. I do not think our courts are well equipped in terms of resources, attitude, or experience to respond sufficiently to the needs of poor people.

With regard to legislatures, the problem—and I think it poses a dire threat to the viability of American democracy—is whether or not the legislatures can respond to the needs of what may well be a permanent minority. The legislature is majority government. The Constitution protects minority rights, but the issue is whether or not, if the poor are to be a permanent minority, legislatures will be interested, assiduous, and alert to providing the opportunities for poor people to lead full lives. If past experience is any guide, they are not prepared to do this sufficiently and with speed.

On top of that, the financial demands on our governments—state, city, and Federal—are so enormous that increasingly legislators are confronted with the idea of taxing themselves to give to the poor. Since we already begin with a fairly high tax base—although it is much lower than what is found in European countries—resistance is building up against taxing ourselves at a still higher rate to give additional monies to the poor. There are no other basic solutions apart from money. I am not, therefore, very optimistic about the long-range prospects, or even the short-range prospects, of change within our legislatures or our court systems.

Ultimately law is not a solution to the problems of the poor; money is. Whatever lawyers do, they do not give the poor money except very indirectly. As a matter of fact, the claim has been made that the poverty programs would be more effective if, instead of giving money to the lawyers who serve the poor, they gave it directly to the poor. However questionable that proposal may seem, the fact remains that the poor will not ultimately achieve power or a solution to their problems through lawyers; they will achieve power only through having money and through having the power which money gives.

9

Mobilization For Youth: Reflections About Its Administration

Bertram M. Beck

All administrators of sizable organizations must frequently make decisions without full knowledge of all the facts involved. Because of the many facets of Mobilization's program, its history, and my own particular style and limitations, I am acutely aware of how little I know of what went on. When I came to Mobilization in 1965, it was a complex organization, with each program-unit head exercising considerable autonomy and without much in the way of written procedures to govern the day-to-day handling of business. Since there was considerable doubt that two of the major money sources, the Ford Foundation and the City of New York, would continue in the partnership, I was forced to deal with the immediate financial crisis, and for the next two and one half years my major effort went into the maintenance of the organization's fiscal stability. When I was not engaged with the problem of maintaining the flow of money, I was handling critical incidents surrounding personnel, community protests, relationships with persons important to organizational survival, and the evolution of the overall program. I found little time actually to see the program or to take a major role in shaping it.

My impressions of the administration of MFY before my arrival are derived in part from the situation I had to deal with after I got here and in part from comments made by people who were here during the early years. Mobilization was one of the first of the giant inner-city projects. The early days and to some extent all of its days were marked by inadequate space, sometimes inadequate direction, and tension between those responsible for program policy and those whose job it was to implement that policy. In the early years, there was also considerable tension between what was called action, or program, and the research effort. By the time I arrived at Mobilization, the major data gathering had been completed, so that this was not a conflict that I was called upon to handle.

From its inception until shortly before I came, Mobilization had three directors: James McCarthy, administrative director; George Brager, program director; and Richard Cloward, research director. All three had been involved in planning the program. Although the form of administration was unconventional, it seemed to work pretty well. Mr. McCarthy's duties were probably pretty much those that I fulfilled. Mr. Brager had responsibilities very similar to those carried for the last couple of years by my associate, Mr. Dan Morris. Dr. Cloward continued to direct the research effort after my appointment, but has done so from his base at the Research Center at the Columbia University School of Social Work rather than as a co-director of Mobilization.

The three directors at the beginning shared a sense of mission and a sense of optimism. They headed a new and ground-breaking organization which had substantial resources. The involvement of Attorney General Robert Kennedy helped to get the program launched, and the involvement of the late Congressman James Fogarty provided the organization with Congressional influence. The sense of mission was transmitted to the staff, and many persons interested in basic social change were attracted to this new organization. Some who came were disillusioned by the difficulties they encountered in actually getting the programs from paper into action. But it seems reasonable to say that morale during those first years was as high as it ever would be in the history of Mobilization.

During these first years insufficient attention was given to procedures for handling funds, personnel classifications, purchasing, and the like, and this became an issue during the time of the crisis. The heart of the crisis, however, had nothing to do with fiscal management but was obviously related to the social-protest activities which had been conducted in a fashion that left Mobilization without any substantial source of ready protection.

Social Action

Mobilization's political power was severely diminished by the assassination of President Kennedy. The agency's loss of a strong supporter opened the way for many evils, and one of them was the opportunity for Paul Screvane, then president of the city council, to lead the fight against Mobilization while Mayor Wagner was abroad. I do not believe that Mr. Screvane was merely using Mobilization to advance his own career. I suspect that he was truly shocked by the agency's vigorous social-action role at a time when such a course of action seemed quite unusual.

The history of Mobilization is of course a microcosm of the history of efforts to produce social change in America during the years of the agency's existence. As I think back over those years, I am struck by the accelerated pace that marks change in our times. Mobilization was born out of the effort of the established Lower East Side social agencies that deal with delinquency, but it soon left its forebears far behind. The basic approach for funding was made to the Federal government, and this was a precursor of the current tendency to bypass state structure in the solution of urban problems. Federal agencies, always more advanced in thinking than their state counterparts, refused to finance anything that smacked of traditional services. Cloward and Ohlin developed a plan which ultimately took most of the action away from the established agencies. Yet in retrospect the plan was little more than the familiar saturation of a neighborhood with services. There was no real provision for attempts to produce significant social changes that might affect the neighborhood.

The difficulty of producing any significant changes led to the emphasis on neighborhood social action, with the staff taking the major responsibility for leading the neighborhood people. As time passed we received our first practical lesson in the unwillingness of government to supply funds to pay the salaries of persons who are attempting to alter basic political and social institutions. Like so many lessons it took a long time to sink in.

Despite the inherent weaknesses in Mobilization's plan to alter social institutions through a big-time demonstration in a small neighborhood, the plan became the model for similar action projects which received funding through the President's Committee on Juvenile Delinquency. When the Economic Opportunity Act was drafted, many persons who had had some role in respect to Mobilization, including myself, participated in pioneering the Economic Opportunity Program. Thus did Mobilization become the seedbed for the War on Poverty. The War on Poverty was seen by some as the logical development of the civil-rights movement: the provision of vast new opportunities for millions of exiled persons. Yet the War on Poverty, like Mobilization, was essentially service oriented, with an element of community organization to give life to the program.

As the staff of the Office of Economic Opportunity implemented the Congressional provision for the maximum feasible participation of the poor, great emphasis was placed on giving the poor themselves a large share in the conduct of programs. As time passed, the constant whittling away of the community-action program by Congress merely echoed the lesson already taught Mobilization concerning the use of public funds for public agitation. This lesson is reflected in current developments within MFY. The conviction that only the redistribution of wealth can make a significant dent in social pathology has caused me to bring new staff into Mobilization and to reshape the program around the purpose of economic development. Any thought that major social change can be induced through a neighborhood organization is gone; it is plain to me that the future of Mobilization depends in large measure on America's willingness to address economic problems. Of course, it is quite possible that we can again get funds for a five-year demonstration.

This would not signify any real willingness for substantial change; however, at the end of the five years, we could feel quite confident that we would leave behind us a working consumers' or producers' cooperative, individuals with prospects for careers, and at least a few new job openings.

For the social-action dimension, I have begun to look to the voluntary agencies. In addition to serving as executive director of Mobilization, I am now executive director of Henry Street Settlement. When Helen Hall, who was instrumental in launching Mobilization, retired after thirty-four years as executive of Henry Street Settlement, Winslow Carlton, board chairman of both Mobilization and Henry Street, and I discussed the possibilities of merging the two organizations. When the boards of both organizations resisted this notion, I agreed to become director of both. Although I have not yet been able to establish any real working relationship between the two organizations, I think that as Mobilization moves toward economic development, the relationship with Henry Street and some of the other neighborhood centers, with their more intimate neighborhood constituencies, will make a great deal of sense. As it is, Mobilization also tends to serve a particular neighborhood, a neighborhood desperately in need of service. With the cooperation of a sympathetic board, it has been possible to move Henry Street Settlement vigorously toward the organization of the adult Negro and Puerto Rican community. I doubt if this would have been possible seven years ago, for it took the social-action efforts of Mobilization and the Economic Opportunity Program to popularize the notion that doing good for people was not enough and that people had to be helped to participate in the social processes.

Recently a hostile reporter, in an article on Mobilization's seventh birthday, charged me with immorality for conducting a demonstration program which offers services and then withdraws them. I had no hesitancy in pointing out that, while it was disillusioning and painful for people to have a service for a certain number of years and then not have it, they nonetheless derived great benefit from the help received during the years of the demonstration. Youngsters who attended college through Mobilization's higher-education program had their education and in some cases have returned to the community in positions of leadership. Many of the organizations fostered by Mobilization still exist. The basic changes in welfare law and practice achieved by Mobilization affect the whole city and the whole nation, and the fact that Mobilization has the vitality to change and to learn by past errors attests to the strength of the experience.

Funding

During my time at the agency, political connections were of minimal assistance in maintaining funds for Mobilization—that is, political connections where there was actually an exchange of favors or a hope of advancing the position of some elected office-holder. Despite the period of crisis, we were successful in maintaining and expanding the funds available for Mobilization programs in each successive year up until the present year, 1968, the year of transition from Mobilization For Youth to Mobilization for Economic Opportunities. The funds obtained in each year of operation are as follows:

YEARLY BUDGETS

1962–63	$2,873,833.00
1963–64	4,899,361.00
1964–65	5,107,212.00
1965–66	5,630,910.00
1966–67	6,578,208.00
1967–68	5,714,885.00

The two major factors in maintaining the flow of money for the Mobilization operation were Mobilization's reputation for operational capacity and an admixture of professional relationships and friendships, some of which I developed during my tenure at Mobilization and many during my service on the Demonstration Review Panel of the President's Committee on Juvenile Delinquency. In a curious way the crisis was helpful in postcrisis fund raising, for it made Mobilization a public issue and gained for it a reputation for social action which, I think, exceeded the reality. After the crisis, persons of liberal inclination were likely to support Mobilization as a cause. Mobilization's reputation for operational capacity was based primarily on its significant contribution of new ideas, documented in earlier volumes. There can be no quarrel with the evidence of this contribution even though those of us who are close to Mobilization have been concerned with improving the quality of the day-to-day operation.

Mobilization over the years had a number of funding sources which contributed varying amounts to the agency, the most prominent of which are the Office of Economic Opportunity, the National Institute of Mental Health, the President's Committee on Juvenile Delinquency, the Ford Foundation, the City of New York, and the U. S. Department of Labor. Accommodating to their differing fiscal procedures, funding periods, and personnel standards was a constant source of difficulty. The original grants which funded Mobilization were for three and five years. When these expired, all programs were funded on a year-by-year basis, thereby introducing a considerable source of instability into the agency. Funding agencies tend to wait until the last minute to make grant renewals because of their own budgetary problems, and staff who have family responsibilities tend to leave in such situations.

In addition to the difficulty of maintaining a consistent flow of funds into the agency,[1] there has been a chronic problem concerning administrative costs. As a consequence of the controversy during the crisis, the comptroller of the Department of Health, Education and Welfare proposed that each year the administrative costs of the agency—executive offices, fiscal, office services, public relations, occupancy, and personnel—which could not properly be charged to any particular program, should be met by all funding sources on a pro-rata basis. This arrangement was approved, and it worked well as long as the Department of Health, Education and

[1] It is clear that large demonstration projects like Mobilization cannot be operated on a yearly funding basis. Such an agency needs a bulk of funds to be able to maintain its key executive staff. The National Institute of Mental Health provided MFY with such stability for the years 1962–67. This stabilizing role may be a function foundations should assume.

Welfare was a major factor in the finances of Mobilization. When the National Institute of Mental Health terminated its grant in 1967, the other funding sources had difficulty in accepting the formula to which they had subscribed under the leadership of Health, Education and Welfare. They persisted in viewing Mobilization as if it were a university which had voluntary funds it could use to pay administrative costs. Program people, who are particularly obtuse about financial matters, regarded a percentage for administration as some kind of gravy train and something which could be cut arbitrarily. Since any funding source which failed to pay its pro-rated share thereby imposed a greater burden on other funding sources, the application of the simple principle developed by Health, Education and Welfare required endless argument.

A second major financial problem which became acute in fiscal year 1968 resulted from the absence of any cash reserve at Mobilization. As long as we had a major grant from Health, Education and Welfare, with a total sum being paid in advance, we were not in acute need of a cash reserve. As soon as we lost that major grant, we were in the position of a storekeeper who was constantly putting out merchandise on charge and has no quick return of money to meet daily bills. Every payday became crisis day as various agencies were invariably slow in sending money, even though we were operating programs under contract to them. I am now in the process of trying to work out a system whereby various foundations might be willing to guarantee our credit so that we will have a credit line of $500,000 at our bank in lieu of a working reserve.

A third major financial problem at Mobilization had to do with the need for establishing procedures which would prevent embezzlement or inadvertent misuse of public funds. Programs such as Mobilization are extremely vulnerable to accusations of financial wrong-doing. At the time of the crisis, MFY was charged not only with communism, but also with financial mismanagement. It seemed as if those who were bent on crucifying Mobilization turned to the latter accusation when it became apparent that there would be little solid evidence to sustain the accusation of communism.[2]

The vulnerability of these programs springs from the fact that often much more attention is given to the program goals than to the more mundane matters of systems and procedures. Recently the importance of hiring neighborhood residents and victims of racial discrimination has overshadowed the importance of hiring people with the kind of passion for fiscal security that makes them good money managers. Unfortunately, what is important for one group is not necessarily important for the total community, and those who are particularly concerned with sound money management and less concerned with social justice can quickly find allies in reactionary efforts when evidence of misuse of money is encountered. Also, it is quite possible that there is a greater risk of financial mismanagement when one employs persons victimized by discrimination, who have been forced to hustle to survive. However, the kind of hustle in which these survivors engage is often cruder and more easily detected than the more subtle varieties of the dominant middle-class community.

The accusations of embezzlement which were lodged against the executives of Mobilization during the crisis were totally false. For example, Federal auditors had disallowed $300,000 worth of expenditures. Many people assumed this meant that the executives then in the news had somehow pocketed this money. Actually, almost all of this disallowance was concerned with the source to which certain expenditures were charged. In other words, there wasn't even an allegation of embezzlement but a point of interest

[2] At the time I took over as executive director, security was an issue. The board had passed a resolution agreeing to have some kind of name check done on the staff. When I conferred with the city department concerned with such matters, I discovered that a name check without fingerprints was extremely unreliable. There was actually no security check made on anybody at any time after my appointment. In the course of time, most of the six or seven individuals who had been accused of some kind of subversive connections left the staff of their own accord. I actually had nothing to do with their leaving, or really with the death of the Communist issue at Mobilization. This issue diminished in importance at Mobilization as it became less important on the American scene. It was eclipsed by the struggle for equal opportunity and other issues.

only to accountants—as to where the funds should be charged.

During my first few years at Mobilization, I spent a great deal of time dealing with the debris of the crisis. This included not only the impact of the crisis on the staff and board, but also the fact that the records were incomplete, since many had been carried away by various investigators and had not been returned. We were also confronted with the fact of these enormous disallowances; either the Federal government had to recant or Mobilization would go bankrupt, since we had no cash whatsoever to pay the bills which the goverment was refusing to meet.

None of this could have been straightened out without Kal Rothbaum, who had been comptroller at Mobilization from its beginning. After endless hours of negotiation with Federal auditors, he got them to agree that the original disallowance was based on incomplete evidence and to reduce the disallowance ultimately to $8,000.

As almost always happens in such matters, the name of James McCarthy, the original administrative director of MFY, which was blackened by the insinuation of financial mismanagement, never reached the headlines in connection with the ultimate settlement of this and other accusations. The injustice done Mr. McCarthy remains substantially uncorrected.

Life at Mobilization in the beginning was certainly characterized by an absence of attention to details of fiscal management. During the crisis the firm of S. D. Leidesdorf had been employed to recommend systems and procedures for improved management. The original document they produced, which was available upon my appointment, required substantial work before being put into operation. I therefore induced Ruth Becker, who had for almost ten years been comptroller at the National Association of Social Workers, to join me at Mobilization. Under her able direction, the original Leidesdorf document evolved into a manual that is a model for organizations like Mobilization. After completing this work, she carried us through the very difficult period of computerizing our financial operations.

Unfortunately, for an agency using public funds, it is not really possible to strike a balance between the risk of embezzlement or error and the flexibility that is desirable for a free and innovative program. The fiscal procedures at Mobilization, particularly in the first two years after I came here, were costly. Even when we reduced the cost, these procedures did not permit program staff the kind of freedom that I would think desirable, yet it was plain to me that organizational survival depended upon our being Caesar's wife. The program staff and the clientele of the agency naturally do not see this in the same light as I do. There has consequently been considerable tension between the people who operate the fiscal services and others involved in the Mobilization program. The issue is complicated by the fact that the mind set of persons drawn to accounting is usually quite different from that of people who are interested in developing programs directed to social change.

Staff Unionization

Most of Mobilization's annual budget goes into salary. Salaries have increased each year with the renegotiation of the union contract. The union chapter received its contract during the time of crisis in 1964. It was symptomatic of the deterioration of relationships between the line staff and the management at that time that, while Winslow Carlton, chairman of the board of Mobilization, was fighting for the life of the organization, he was picketed by the staff seeking a union contract. Because at the time the contract was negotiated nobody could give substantial time to the matter and the future of the agency was so problematical, the union chapter gained from Mobilization a contract which was absurdly ill-suited to the nature of the agency. This has constituted a severe handicap to the successful maintenance of the organization.

The contract was written as if Mobilization had control of its own funds, an indefinite future, and an endowment. Completely ignored was fact that Mobilization receives funds for a particular program for a twelve-month period and that any funds not expended are returned to the source of funds. The contract is based on the assumption that Mobilization can determine how much it's going to pay people and then pay them. In fact, the amount that can be paid is determined largely by the source of funds. The contract calls for the payment of liberal severance benefits, and yet when I came to Mobilization, no provision had been made for accumulation of a reserve fund to pay any severance benefits. For all practical purposes, it is impossible to reduce benefits once they are given, and within that framework I think we did pretty well in negotiating the two contracts to which I was a party after coming to Mobilization. The last contract was for a two-year period and will be renegotiated for July 1, 1969. For this next contract I hope to receive sanction from the board of directors to take an extremely firm position in respect to achieving modifications in the contract that reflect the way in which funds for Mobilization are secured and administered.

In the course of union negotiations at Mobilization, I basically altered some of the personnel policies. When I came to Mobilization, there was a very primitive job classification which divided jobs into professional, semiprofessional, administrative, clerical, and the like. A new system was developed in 1965 whose major feature was the abolition of the semiprofessional category. This was reflected through the establishment of some six different grades of social worker, all bearing the title "social worker." The underlying concept was that there is no semiprofessional job in social work, that the quality of the intervention of the social worker depends upon the knowledge and skill he brings to that intervention. Under this plan, pay is granted for competent performance, and competence is judged not by the possession of a credential but by the ability to perform.

Although the concept still seems sound, it is unfortunately, in our present state of ignorance, impossible to implement. We never were successful in adequately describing the hierarchy of tasks that would differentiate the social worker six from the social worker one. As a consequence, everyone who lacked the master's degree tended to begin at social worker one, and all those who had the master's degree started at social worker four.

During my time at the agency we never had any systematic training program. Thus, whether persons without formal education picked up new knowledge and skill was dependent entirely upon the quality of their supervisor. At one point I developed a plan in conjunction with three accredited schools of social work whereby, over a five-year period, we might attempt systematically to bring a group of community residents without substantial formal education to the level of competence of the beginning social worker with a master's degree. This plan attracted substantial interest but I never found the time to develop it fully. I still plan to try. It seems plain to me that a university credential plan discriminates against those for whom the educational system does not work. Yet a solution cannot be found by knocking education and romanticizing the contribution to social services of persons whose work is based on folk wisdom and intuition. Obviously, there must be some other route to gaining expertise than university training.

In some respects the presence of the union at Mobilization has undoubtedly been good for the organization. Most important, it has forced attention to injustices done to staff members which would not be corrected without the ardent advocacy of the union. Yet for a demonstration project, a union presents real difficulties, especially in the restrictions it places on retrenching employees who are unable to meet the demands of innovation and demonstration as projects change and develop.

Mobilization as "Establishment"

Throughout its history, Mobilization has, of course, been strongly influenced by social developments in the nation at large. When it was instituted, the key leadership at Mobilization quite properly viewed MFY as the cutting edge and were inclined to be scornful of traditional social agencies. By the time five years had elapsed, Mobilization itself was viewed as "establishment." Although it may be that the vigorous social-action posture of Mobilization prior to the crisis was so tempered that the community's view of the agency changed, I think that the change in perception was more closely associated with changes in the community itself than with anything that happened at Mobilization. The original board of directors at Mobilization was composed largely of power figures in the city and on the Lower East Side. The idea was that, if you got representatives of all the different social institutions to the table, changes in those institutions might be effected. When the crisis came, there was evident conflict of interests for representatives of public agencies serving on the Mobilization Board. Almost all these members of the board resigned by joint agreement, leaving a nucleus to reconstruct the board. The new board continued to include representation of some of the religious organizations and settlement houses on the Lower East Side. However, it was largely composed of midtown attorneys, sociologists, union leaders, and the like. In short, it was in many ways an ideal board for Mobilization, since the board has had no fund-raising function, and knowledge of public policy was the most valuable ingredient that most board members could bring.

When the new board was set up, there was some discussion of adding program participants as members. Ultimately it was decided to add them to board committees, with the notion that persons from the committees would gradually be added to the board. When one considers how conservative that approach appears three years later, one realizes how swift has been the development of the notion of consumer participation in the past few years. In time, the requirements of the Office of Economic Opportunity accelerated the process, and one third of the board became persons from the neighborhood, largely drawn from the poorer sector of the neighborhood.

Since neighborhood residents who participated actively in the board tended to be more faithful in their attendance than active midtown people, the attendance at board meetings tended to be comprised of about 40 percent neighborhood residents and about 60 percent directors of local settlements, local clergymen, and the midtown group. After some initial awkwardness a modus operandi was established. The midtown people allowed the neighborhood residents "to do their thing" and vice versa. The neighborhood residents were given to militant rhetoric and to attempts to use the board to solve problems with which they were personally concerned. The midtown method consisted of controlled, directed discussion and voting on items on a prepared agenda.

The need for some plan of operation became apparent to me later when I became active in the New York Urban Coalition. There considerable tension was engendered because of the difference in styles of participation between the community representatives and the corporate representatives. The community representatives complained that there was no problem solving at the meetings, only "voting." The corporate representatives complained that there was too much talk. One corporate president announced that he never allowed a meeting to go over one hour when he was chairman. A community representative replied by pointing out that neighborhood meetings are invariably an hour late in getting started and barely get going in two or three hours.

About a year ago I proposed to a staff meeting that Mobilization be reconstituted as a membership corporation, with membership open to any resident of the Lower East Side. The members would then be eligible to elect a board of directors. There was very little enthusiasm for this proposal. Experience has demonstrated to me that staff members who are most vehement in calling for community control actually do not want to work under a board composed of neighborhood residents who will take an active part in influencing personnel practices in the agency. In three instances, when segments of Mobilization program were transferred to the control of a community board, the staff of the program vigorously or covertly resisted the move. Persons who are not part of the middle-class tradition of board membership do not accept the traditional distinctions between board functions and executive functions. This has been the experience throughout the antipoverty program. The traditional board member of the classical social agency tends to be wealthier than the people employed by the agency and to have little interest in influencing personnel policies. When neighborhood residents become board members, they are very much interested in the salaries of persons on the staff and quite naturally seek positions for themselves or their friends or relatives. In a situation such as pertains at Mobilization, where middle-class people are the executives and many low-income neighborhood residents are on the staff, a neighborhood residents' board will be much quicker to control salaries and take disciplinary action in respect to staff than will the middle-class executives.

Had low-income neighborhood residents dominated the board of Mobilization, either the organization would have come to an end or board composition would have made little difference. If the board had sought to replace top-level executives, it is doubtful that funding for Mobilization would have continued. Unlike most antipoverty programs, Mobilization has obtained funds not because of the social or political power of a particular ethnic group, but only because of its operational capacity plus the confidence of those who give funds in the top Mobilization staff.[3] If there had been a board of neighborhood low-income residents who did not replace the top-level staff, the organization would have continued pretty much along the road it has traveled, since that road has been determined largely by the interaction between the top-level staff and the funding sources, with the board having minimal control.

Despite my perception of Mobilization's necessary tie with middle-class leadership, pressure on Mobilization as an organization of the establishment increased with the growth of the anti-poverty program and the civil-rights revolution. With the formation of the Community Corporation (in part a consequence of my efforts to see that there was a genuinely representative community group to control antipoverty funds), Mobilization became the target for a great deal of anger and hostility. The Community Corporation was largely dominated by the Puerto Rican group, and

[3] Mobilization was able to survive because its funds for research and demonstration came directly from Washington, rather than filtered through city poverty agencies. Nevertheless, the agency could never have been maintained both before and after the public attack on it without the loyal support of the board. The dedication and concern of the citizens, rich and poor, professional and nonprofessional, not only legitimated the agency but also served as a useful check on the viability of program proposals. The reader is commended to a list of their names appended to this volume.

they saw Mobilization as an organization without many Puerto Ricans in top leadership and thus without a close and sympathetic relationship to the neighborhood in which it functioned. Aggravating the hostilities that grew out of these perceptions was the tendency which developed all over the city of giving vent to frustration and hostility by attacking dominant local organizations, even though the root sources of social dislocation were more distant, more powerful, and more complex.

The situation was not helped by my well-publicized criticisms of the antipoverty program on the ground that it stressed the participation of the poor and the conduct of service-delivery programs rather than economic development of the neighborhood which would bring people into effective social and political participation. I also publicly criticized the failure of the poverty program to advance coalition between different ethnic and economic groups. I supported what was to most liberal political figures and most anti-poverty officials the "notorious" Green amendment, which mandated coalition in the management of antipoverty programs. I also criticized community poverty elections as diverting attention from the overall political situation and establishing competition among shut-out indigenous groups for the peanuts of the antipoverty program while larger forces in society split the big melon.

The local critics of Mobilization perceived the organization in a much different light. This led to many confrontations. Certainly the essence of the administrative job at any organization like Mobilization these days is the handling of confrontation. At times I was confronted directly by neighborhood residents and at times by members of the Mobilization staff. Few of my confrontations with participants actually concerned a critique of Mobilization. Any resentment about the administration of Mobilization was implicit. Confrontations usually concerned money matters.

There were a whole series of explosive meetings with neighborhood residents being trained as social workers in cooperation with Beth Israel Hospital. A number of Mobilization's staff members were closely identified with the trainees and viewed MFY and Beth Israel as repressive and unsympathetic. To complicate the situation, the first group of trainees included some of the more militant neighborhood residents. The encounters concerned my attempt to fire one of the MFY staff members, the salaries offered trainees upon completion of training, the positions being offered them at that time, and various other matters.

A great deal of accidental learning came out of these difficult sessions. At the time, I was extremely annoyed by the role of the staff in encouraging the trainees' activities. I believe the administration at Beth Israel was even more annoyed, and found the trainees a very difficult group to assimilate into program. In retrospect, however, I think that the trainees' urge to resist bureaucratic control, aided and abetted by the antiestablishment MFY staff, was very valuable. It is likely that MFY might have acquiesced to the claim of Beth Israel that they couldn't find jobs for the trainees if the trainees themselves hadn't protested. The professional has some inoculation against being entirely dehumanized, because his professional training acts as a counterbalance to institutional brainwashing. The experience of "winning" at Beth Israel enabled the trainees to enter their permanent positions with a sense of their own power and dignity. While I cannot establish cause and effect here, it is certainly true that these trainees have made absolutely phenomenal records. A substantial number, on their own momentum, have gone on to obtain high-school equivalency diplomas and are hoping to enter college.[4]

Another notable confrontation with neighborhood residents concerned the desire of an organization called the Negro Federation to continue their program, or at least to enlarge their program, at a time when Mobilization did not have funds to increase their sub-

[4] In October 1966, Mobilization began operation of a New Health Occupations Program under funds provided jointly by Office of Manpower Policy, Evaluations and Research of the U. S. Department of Labor and the Office of Economic Opportunity. Three groups of twenty low-income residents of the Lower East Side were trained as Social Health Technicians, a new occupation in health services, to assist social workers and public-health nurses in carrying out their duties. An evaluation of this program can be found in Final Report to the Office of the Associate Manpower Administrator, U. S. Department of Labor, OAMA Contract No. 82-34-66-25 (mimeographed, New York, Mobilization For Youth, August 30, 1968).

contracts. The confrontation began with a picket line on the day of a board meeting. I invited the group to send representatives to the meeting, and for many board members this was a very unusual experience. At least one member of the federation group had been drinking, possibly to bolster her courage. The meeting with the board was loud and angry, and still the board was moved by the dramatic testimony of the need for a day-care center for which the federation was seeking funds.

After wrestling with the problem of what would happen if we did try to give in to this one organization without taking care of the others with which we had contracts, we decided to cut down on other activities at Mobilization to the amount of $60,000 and then ask all eight of the local organizations with which we had contracts to decide themselves how they wanted to allot this amount. This, of course, turned out to be a difficult process, but in the long run it was productive, and I think all of the groups were strengthened in their ability to deal with one another and with Mobilization.

The production of the $60,000 under pressure reinforced the notion that Mobilization could find money any time it wanted to. This led to a series of very active demonstrations by both staff and neighborhood whenever a program was threatened. In most instances, I did find some way of getting money for the program and again confirmed a view of Mobilization as too powerful. Of course there came a time when this failed, and it occurred when we lost our city tax funding in 1968. The youngsters in our education program and their teachers made a wonderful effort to save the program, through petitions and appearances at the city council and the board of directors. I was convinced from the beginning that this time there was no hope of saving the program, yet I didn't feel I could do other than go along with the efforts of staff and program participants. Apparently there are some occasions in these collective-action efforts when speaking the truth only heightens the frustrations of those who seek action, and I had to decide whether to go along with a series of actions that I felt were futile or, by refusing, become the target myself. I chose not to become the target, but I was not comfortable with the decision.

A direct confrontation with staff occurred around the question of the ethnicity of top management after I had retrenched the director of Community Development, an able Negro woman who had been with Mobilization since the very beginning. A group of staff members, most of them Negroes with some Puerto Rican representation, petitioned me, met with me, and wrote letters to the boards of many local organizations and even to the funding sources. I have no quarrel with their request that there be more black and Puerto Rican people in top leadership posts at Mobilization, but their facts were usually wrong, and I found myself in disagreement with their specific demands. For example, their key demand centered around the fact that I had appointed a "nonminority person" as assistant director for research and development. They believe that the director of Community Development could have done the job. I did not. This went again to the fact that the only way I saw to maintain Mobilization was to maintain its operational capacity.

During my first months at Mobilization, I found myself so pressed by other matters, I did not give sufficient attention to key staff appointments. After the confrontation I did make a very careful attempt to bring blacks and Puerto Ricans into top positions. There were plenty of qualified people, but they were in great demand. One of the points made by the dissident staff members was that we didn't have enough black attorneys. Yet, every time we hired a black attorney, he was hired right out from under us at a substantial salary increase with which we couldn't compete. Actually, over my years at Mobilization the number of blacks and Puerto Ricans among the executive staff has subtantially increased. I am sure it is not large enough, but given the context in which we operate, I believe it's the best that could have been done.

Behind many confrontations with neighborhood residents is the implicit threat of violence. The administrator does not want to let the situation develop into one where he or the protesters will have to use force. On the other hand, one is constrained to represent the reality and not merely give in to any group that presses lest one stimulate still more collective activity of this sort. Yet consistent denials stimulate greater anger.

Most of the decisions I made under this kind of pressure seem to me in retrospect to be the best decisions that I could have made. Yet I doubt very much that they contributed to any real improvement in the social order. Many of these confrontations are actually between a deprived group and a liberal. There is a large element of play-acting, a great deal of discharge of energy which makes the happening an end in itself. Nobody learns from this experience how reactionary power behaves.

Since it is obvious that society is not ready to make the substantial redress of grievances that is necessary, the happenings that go on in the name of social action in the antipoverty arena are a tragic sideshow in which I felt forced by circumstances to participate. Militant action certainly has a place when the disinherited confront their real enemies. When it takes place in the context of the antipoverty effort, it merely serves to dissipate energy. Had the nation been genuinely interested in abolishing poverty, the War on Poverty would have had an economic base and would have led to some redistribution of wealth with a consequent redistribution of power.

One final note about administration is in order. Through my years at Mobilization I have been assisted by Val Coleman as director of public relations. His ability to merge public relations and program has been a major factor not only in the success of many programs but also in projecting the character of Mobilization so that continued support for it could be maintained. Phillip Selznick has said:

> The character of an organization may be regarded as the product of its ingrained methods of work, its natural allies, its stake in the course of events, the predispositions of its personnel, and the labels (deserved and undeserved) which have become attached to it. These characteristics reflect the organization's controlling roles and pur-

poses; they generate those established patterns of expectation with which the organization is uniquely identified.[5]

They also determine whether it will live or die. At this juncture Mobilization is very much alive and concerned with developing the economic side of its character. Only time will tell if this is a wise development. And even if it is not, it is in the best tradition of a noble effort to innovate and help, which was and is Mobilization For Youth.

[5] Phillip Selznick, *The Organizational Weapon* (New York, McGraw-Hill, 1952), p. 56.

10

Politics and Planning: Mobilization as a Model

Frances Fox Piven

Since the early 1960's, a new pattern of Federal-local relations has taken form, entailing direct intervention by the Federal government in services to local neighborhoods, especially ghetto neighborhoods. Several major pieces of legislation have been enacted, each enlarging the scope of Federal intervention. In 1961 the Juvenile Delinquency and Youth Offenses Control Act was passed, authorizing the expenditure of $10 million for grants to youth development projects for the prevention and treatment of juvenile delinquency. In 1963 the Community Mental Health Centers Act authorized $150 million to finance community centers which would serve as the nucleus for what President Kennedy called a "bold new approach" to the prevention and treatment of mental illness. In 1964 Title II of the Economic Opportunity Act allocated $350 million to community action programs which, in President Johnson's words, would "strike at poverty at its source—in the streets of our cities and on the farms of our countryside . . . calling on all resources available to the community—Federal and State, local and private, human and material." In 1965, under Title I of the Elementary and Secondary Education Act, $1 billion was allocated for a variety of projects and services to disadvantaged children. And in 1966, Title I of the Demonstration Cities and Metropolitan Development Act called for a "comprehensive attack on social, economic, and physical problems in selected slum and blighted areas through the most effective and economical concentration and coordination of Federal, State, and local public and private efforts . . . to develop 'model' neighborhoods."

Each of these measures was proposed as a way of dealing with a distinctive social problem, presumably requiring a distinctive strategy of amelioration. Yet, despite the variety of advertised social problems and legislative titles—delinquency, mental health, poverty, model cities—the major programs for the cities have remarkable similarities. First, all provide a wide variety of services, from unemployment programs to family counseling. Second, under the broad umbrella of community development, all carve out local neighborhoods in the urban ghettos as service areas. Most important, all these enactments represent a new pattern of Federal-local relations.

What has to be explained is why this new pattern has emerged. Why, in response to trouble in the cities, has the Federal government begun to intervene directly in services for poor communities instead of merely expanding existing grant-in-aid programs which channeled money through state and municipal agencies? To understand this, one must go beyond the legislative rationales of the different programs to the political context in which these measures were launched.

Political Imperatives

The new pattern of Federal action is commonly justified by the need to deal with various acute urban problems, problems so massive that the cities have been unable to cope with them, for lack of both local revenues and local competence. Thus, we hear that the urban physical environment has so deteriorated that the Federal government has been forced to launch programs to improve housing and neighborhoods. Other programs are needed to deal with service breakdowns: the failure of the schools, inadequate health services, and most recently and urgently the breakdown of law and order.

But few of these conditions are new, nor is it even clear that most of them are worsening. The city has always had slums, and there is less overcrowding today than ever before. Services in education and health have probably improved, even for the poorest people in the city. And we have had periods of widespread violence at other times in our history. The severity of urban problems apparently does not account for the rash of Federal activity in the cities, and surely not for the curiously similar features of the manifestly different programs. In any case, traditional grant-in-aid programs already provided the vehicles, if not the funds, to deal with these problems.

It is the thesis of this chapter that these new programs are largely a response to new political imperatives. Underlying the elaborations about urban problems were certain critical problems which the new Democratic Administration confronted in 1960. The victory had been a narrow one, and it seemed to bring to the forefront important changes in the party constituency. The South had once more defected, confirming what had been becoming clear throughout the 1950's—that the South could no longer be counted as "solid." (Mississippi and Alabama went States Rights; Florida, Tennessee, Kentucky, and Virginia voted Republican.) President Kennedy owed his victory to the heavy Democratic vote in key cities, and especially to the black vote in those cities. He slid through in Illinois by 8,000 votes, a margin that was the result of landslide majorities in the black southside wards of Chicago.

Kennedy's good showing in the northern ghettos was no simple reflection of party reliability. The widespread defection of Negroes to Eisenhower (39% in 1956) had made it clear that the black vote could by no means be taken for granted. Rather, the ghettos were responding to the fact that Kennedy had campaigned on a strong civil rights platform, as Stevenson had not done in either 1952 or 1956. It was with these experiences in clear view that the new Administration began to explore ways to cement the allegiance of the black vote in the cities.

Although it was important to hold and increase those black votes, the Kennedy Administration faced severe problems in following through on its civil rights commitments. Civil rights legislation was sure to meet fierce resistance from Southerners in the Congress (where a coalition of southern Democrats and Republicans were in any case to make trouble for the President's overall legislative program), and civil rights legislation was likely also to fan the racism of the white working classes, already becoming a divisive factor in Democratic urban constituencies.[1] Alternative ways of placating the urban ghetto vote were needed.

The new Administration turned to a series of service programs for the inner city, where blacks were concentrated. First to be launched were multimillion-dollar juvenile delinquency projects in the inner cores of sixteen cities, followed in rapid succession by measures for community mental health, poverty, education, and physical redevelopment (model cities). These programs were in part designed to generate, hold, and increase ghetto votes, but not at the expense of further alienating whites from the party. How were these dual requirements to be achieved?

For building party loyalty among blacks, the new Federal programs featured a battery of services not unlike those offered by the old-time political club: jobs or access to jobs, training or access to training, and access to a host of public services.[2] Also like the old-time community-based political club were the neighborhood offices and storefronts through which the Federal programs were to be carried out, offices where "advocates" could help residents avail themselves of the services of city agencies and even challenge the rulings of these agencies.[3] Thus, social workers could badger wel-

[1] The Civil Rights Act of 1964 was not submitted until February 1963, after Kennedy's position had been strengthened by an unprecedented midterm victory. Until then he did very little, aside from signing an Executive Order banning discrimination in Federally subsidized housing (which he did nothing to implement) and backing a bill to ease voter literacy requirements.

[2] For a more extensive analysis of the Federal strategy for the inner cities, see a paper written by the author with Richard A. Cloward, "Urban Disruption and the Consolidation of National Power," *Urban Riots: Violence and Social Change,* The Proceedings of the Academy of Political Science, Vol. 29, No. 1 (August 1968).

[3] A more detailed description of the uses of advocacy may be found in a paper by the author, "Advocacy as a Strategy of Political Management," *Perspecta 12; Yale Architectural Review* (Fall 1968).

fare departments to put people on the rolls and harass housing inspectors until they act; lawyers could dispute evictions and contest police actions; advocate planners could counter city redevelopment plans with alternate plans prepared with neighborhood groups. The political function of this kind of activity is not only to help the residents directly, but also to stimulate regular city agencies to greater responsiveness to ghetto dwellers. In these respects, the national Administration was employing the traditional political strategy of offering a market basket of favors to encourage adherence to the party.

The problem of reaching black voters in the cities has been greatly complicated, however, by the need to avoid antagonizing whites. White ethnic blocs, while depleting in numbers, are still the major Democratic constituents in the cities. Their hostility to the growing numbers of blacks in the cities was already apparent in 1960, and any new concession to the ghetto might aggravate it further.

One device that the Federal programs evolved to deal with this problem is the community development approach. By defining the ghetto as the locus of activity—whether the activity is intended to combat mental illness, juvenile delinquency, poverty, or whatever— this approach minimizes the possibility of conflict with whites. The emphasis is on redeveloping the ghetto, which is reassuring to whites who fear that blacks might overrun their neighborhoods and schools.

To implement this strategy of ghetto community development, the Administration had to contend with the apparatus of city government, which in most places was likely to resist the redirection of any services to blacks. Merely to increase grants-in-aid intended for the ghetto would not do, for the cities were likely to use such funds to serve the groups to whom they were already tied—often at the expense of blacks as the history of public housing and urban renewal had already shown.[4] If the ghetto voters were to be

---

[4] These programs set the precedent for direct relations between the Federal government and city agencies. But local housing authorities often failed to use even the small funds allocated to them for public housing, and urban renewal agencies became notorious for their ready accommodation

reached by new Federal programs, city government had somehow to be circumvented; the existing methods of giving grants-in-aid had to be changed.[5] But while local agencies had to be circumvented or redirected, their collaboration was also essential. Without it, not only were the Federal programs likely to be obstructed, but the Federal strategy would have backfired, cultivating the support of blacks only to alienate municipal agencies—and their white constituencies.[6] This ticklish political problem of somehow intervening in the pattern of services to ghetto communities while maintaining the collaboration of local agencies shaped much of the Federal activity for the urban ghetto.

The first of the new Federal programs to be launched was in delinquency prevention, and the first local project created under it, Mobilization For Youth, was located on the Lower East Side of New York City. The remainder of this chapter describes the process of Federal intervention in municipal service patterns which underlay the Mobilization project. The problems involved in such intervention, and the outlines of a strategy to deal with them, were already apparent in this early venture.

The Early Design

The Administration began gropingly; all that was clear at first was that there should be some kind of program for the inner city.

to local business interests. See Martin Anderson, *The Federal Bulldozer,* Cambridge: MIT Press, 1964. Herbert Gans, "The Failure of Urban Renewal," *Commentary,* April 1965, pp. 29–37; and Chester Hartman, "The Housing of Relocated Families," *Journal of the American Institute of Planners,* Vol. 30, No. 4 (November 1964), pp. 266–86.

[5] For a description of the emergence of direct Federal-city funding relations in the 1930's and 1940's in the context of prevailing Federal-state granting patterns, see Roscoe C. Martin, *The Cities and the Federal System,* New York: Atherton Press, 1965.

[6] This dilemma is vividly represented in the wording of the Economic Opportunities Act of 1964, which requires "maximum feasible participation" of the poor (a tactic to stimulate responsiveness in local agencies); and, at the same time also requires the inclusion of political, business, labor, and religious leaders, the school board, the employment service, the public-welfare department, private social agencies, and neighborhood settlement houses.

But the emergence of delinquency as a primary focus was not accidental. Mounting crime rates in the city were widely reported in the press and featured as a problem by an array of civic groups.[7] More important, crime in the streets was becoming the focus of tension between major urban voting blocs, particularly between white ethnic groups and black newcomers. Indeed, conflict between black and white was growing so intense that programs designed to placate one or the other of these contending groups were being mangled. Public housing, for example, because it was associated with the black poor, had aroused so much opposition from whites (particularly when projects made incursions into white neighborhoods) that it had come to a virtual standstill in many cities.

By contrast, the delinquency problem seemed an especially promising issue around which to frame a Federal program. It held out the promise of new services to blacks and, simultaneously, the promise of law and order to whites. The very services which would appeal to the swelling numbers in the ghettos would also assuage the whites who feared the ghettos.

Initiating Collaboration

For a new strategy for the cities to be implemented, a collaborative network had to be established among a wide range of agencies, Federal and local, public and private. The diverse service resources of these agencies were needed to make the clubhouse approach effective; and in any case, their political support was needed if the strategy was not to be obstructed.

Collaboration on the Federal Level

The first move came shortly after the election of 1960. The

[7] According to Federal reports, the national rate of reported juvenile court delinquency had doubled in the previous decade. See *Report to the Congress on Juvenile Delinquency,* prepared jointly by the National Institute of Mental Health, National Institute of Health, Public Health Service, and Children's Bureau, Social Security Administration, U. S. Department of Health, Education and Welfare, January 1960, p. 5.

President's Committee on Juvenile Delinquency and Youth Crime was established by Executive Order and directed to coordinate the various Federal activities in delinquency. As an initial instrument of Federal Action, the committee was so structured as to assure it several advantages. It was headed by Attorney General Robert Kennedy, and so would be responsive to the White House. It also included the Secretary of the Department of Health, Education, and Welfare and the Secretary of the Department of Labor, and so could hope to draw on a range of existing agencies that controlled funds and programs which could presumably be redirected to the new inner city ventures. The committee device also made possible at least a liaison relationship with the agencies which had come to think of delinquency as their own terrain. The first task of the committee was to draft new legislation and oversee its passage through the Congress.

For six years during the 1950's, prodded by the Federal agencies with stakes in delinquency activity, the Congress had held hearings on delinquency legislation. As one observer remarked, "Delinquency was like sin, always good for a hearing. . . . Mayor Wagner would bring down his suitcase full of knives and other weapons taken from gang members—I think he just left the suitcase here each year and opened it up at the hearing." But while the Congress was becoming alert to the delinquency problem, the proposed legislation had little spark and acquired no important political support. It called for Federal aid to state and local communities to support increased facilities and staffs—that is, for more funds to be expended through traditional agencies on various ongoing and parochial activities.

The first signs of congressional movement in response to delinquency came from a Subcommittee of the House Appropriations Committee, headed by Representative John Fogarty, Democrat from Rhode Island. Representative Fogarty called on the Children's Bureau and the National Institute of Mental Health (NIMH) to prepare reports on the delinquency problem. The committee responded with some new appropriations, the larger part of which went to the more prestigious NIMH.

The real political push, however, came with the new Administration of 1960. With the Attorney General taking the lead in mobilizing congressional support, legislation was soon enacted permitting the federal funding of 16 pilot delinquency programs in local communities.[8] The first of these, as we have noted, was Mobilization For Youth on New York's Lower East Side.

Collaboration Among Agencies in the Local Neighborhood

The new Federal program found a vast array of local organizations, in a sense, ready and waiting. The mounting rates of delinquency in the 1950's were coming into focus in the city governments, the universities, and the local neighborhoods. To hundreds of agencies in scores of cities the delinquency problem seemed an opportunity for the expansion of their organizational activities. It was these organizations with which the Federal government would have to deal in pursuing its strategy of intervention and collaboration, and the innumerable accommodations with these agencies helped to shape the youth development projects which finally emerged. The Mobilization For Youth venture was not a simple act of the new Administration. Rather, it was the culmination of negotiations and accommodations among an array of Federal and local groups whose first stirring on the delinquency problem could be traced back several years.

During the early 1950's, local social agencies on the Lower East Side, particularly the settlement houses, had become increasingly concerned about the fighting gangs which roamed the neighborhood.[9] The settlements and churches had attempted to deal with the problem by sponsoring recreation and counseling projects and by organizing a "community alert" to warn of gang trouble. One

[8] The Juvenile Delinquency and Youth Offenses Control Act of 1961.

[9] Many of the historical observations in this paper draw on evidence collected in an intensive study of Mobilization For Youth, covering the period from 1957, when the project was first conceived, until the fall of 1963, one year after the action program was put into operation. All quotations are taken directly from written memoranda, correspondence, or interviews with participants.

evening in 1957, local agency people met at the Henry Street Settlement House to discuss these various efforts. A Henry Street board member was apparently sufficiently impressed by the urgency of the problem to offer a small grant to explore "what it would take," as one participant put it, "to really do the job."

"What it would take," the Henry Street group decided, was enough money to launch a community-wide program which would "make use of everything we knew to help children and families." Local efforts thus far had been hampered, they felt, by inadequate resources. "The problem now is not so much *how* to do it, since the methods are known; the problem is to find sufficient means to meet the whole problem." [10]

The Henry Street group began to solicit funds from several sources. It received some encouragement from the National Institute of Mental Health, which had been looking for a community laboratory to serve as a testing ground for its new sociological perspective on delinquency. A long period of negotiation ensued between the National Institute of Mental Health and the local groups, during which several proposals were submitted and turned down before the project was finally given planning funds. Throughout this process, various themes were reiterated by members of the NIMH committee. The local agencies should be united in support of the proposals. Relationships should be established with "outside centers of power"—especially with such public institutions as the schools—so as to ensure some transfer of power in the improvement of the community. The proposal should be a means of bringing about innovations in the practice of existing agencies, since innovation was essential if agencies were to once again serve the community. The services introduced by the proposed program should have the potential of becoming indigenous. And something should be done for the Lower East Side, a neighborhood which has contributed so much to America's cultural heritage.

Two conditions were especially stressed, consistent with the

[10] From one of the early Mobilization documents prepared under Henry Street auspices.

National Institute of Mental Health's own organizational perspective. As an agency of government, NIMH was anxious to avoid the political repercussions of the interagency squabbling which had long characterized the Lower East Side, a territory densely settled with social agencies. The community would have to demonstrate its readiness by establishing a firm collaborative structure to receive the money. Henry Street had already begun to try to develop cooperative working relationships with other local institutions on whose territorial prerogatives the Henry Street program infringed. The evolution of a structure for local collaboration was marked by internecine dealings, themselves an elaborate story, revolving around local struggles for dominance. It was clear to the local agency leaders, however, that a cooperative arrangement was necessary if funds were to be granted; and they did in time submit to a collaborative structure.

More important, the National Institute of Mental Health, a research-oriented agency, required that the local project include a research and evaluation component, which would have to be based at a university. While the local practitioners held no particular brief for academic research, NIMH requirements were clear. After initial negotiations with a group at New York University were disrupted by internal struggles among the local agencies, the Columbia University School of Social Work was approached and agreed to prepare a research proposal.

This new linkage shifted the center of influence to the university and seemed also to shift the goals and ideas for program. The university researchers were, as they said themselves, "the ones who could get the money." They shared the NIMH interest in scientific research, and not accidentally, for they were close professional associates of the NIMH advisory committee, which was composed of nationally known academicians and professionals (and in fact included one of the Columbia University researchers).[11]

[11] This was by no means unusual. The National Institute of Mental Health relied on reputable professionals as consultants for its grant decisions. It also sought to make its grants to reputable professionals. The result was that the funders and the funded were in many cases associated or even identical.

The stress on research meant that whatever action programs were developed should lend themselves to research evaluation; research and action, as one of the committee members said, "should test each other." Service programs should be derived from the theoretical underpinnings of the research, and the success of these services should be susceptible to research evaluation.[12] In concrete terms this meant that the local Mobilization group would have to undergo an extended research and planning period during which suitable new proposals would be developed, and during which the university researchers would have a great deal to say about the formulation of service programs.

The resulting proposal, prepared with an NIMH planning grant (and later funded by the President's Committee, the Ford Foundation, and the City of New York), was put forward in terms of the delinquency and opportunity perspective. It stressed the importance of programs to improve educational and work opportunities in the neighborhood. The initial Henry Street group had taken quite another view and stressed quite different programs. The improvement of behavior, they said, "calls for the skilled use of personal contact through face-to-face methods"—that is, for the direct services in counseling and recreation which settlements have traditionally provided. But, others of their views were not inconsistent with the Columbia opportunity-theory perspective. They had described their neighborhood as one in which "the horizon is limited . . . where there are poor prospects for social or economic advancement." Such notions eased for them the shift that was demanded by the National Institute of Mental Health and to which they acceded, for services of any kind would bring them funds.

The Collaboration Among Municipal Agencies

Various other groups and organizations were also moving in response to the opportunities presented by the delinquency prob-

12 This account is based on the reports of several people who were present at the deliberations of the National Institute of Mental Health Ad Hoc Review Committee.

lem. The New York City Youth Board had been founded in the late 1940's to do street work with delinquency-prone youth, as well as to provide the usual assortment of services in group work, family counseling, and community organization. The Youth Board had also been charged with the coordination of all other youth services in the city. This, however, was a formal prerogative. The Board had no capacity to implement it in the face of the vast array of existing organizations that provided services to youth, each of which was anxious to protect its jurisdiction against any "coordinator," and some of which indeed claimed the role of coordinator for their own.

At the same time, the City Administrator's Office, also formally charged with coordination, and also without the resources and authority to coordinate, was searching for a public issue and program around which to make a bid for increased powers. Delinquency might be such an issue, and services to children and youth might be such a program. Still, the kinds of recommendations then being put forward by different agencies, each merely stressing the expansion of its own parochial services, could not provide the rationale for the comprehensive jurisdiction the City Administrator's Office was seeking to develop.

As gang delinquency mounted in the 1950's, various civic groups began to express concern, and fastened on the apparent lack of coordination of services for children and youth, an issue which was in part created for them by the two city agencies involved. Mayor Wagner responded by commissioning a study, as mayors are inclined to do when competing claims create a political dilemma. The findings of that study also called for coordination, but questioned the claim of the Youth Board to this role on the ground that it was administratively unsound to expect an operating agency to coordinate the activities of other agencies. Still, study reports are suffered easily, especially in New York City, and no action seemed imminent.

A protest from a group of Harlem leaders precipitated a decision, however, among the competing claims of the Youth Board, the City Administrator's Office, and other youth-serving agencies.

In 1961, the Youth Board, together with the Jewish Board of Guardians and the Community Mental Health Board, had initiated a psychiatric street-work project in Harlem. Bolstered by the new concern for Negro rights, the Harlem group took affront at this fresh display of "social-welfare colonialism." No Harlem leaders had been consulted, and no Harlem agencies had been included. The group took its protest to the Mayor a week before election. Squirming to evade this new assault, the Mayor turned to the City Administrator's Office and charged it to begin forthwith the coordination of youth services.

The City Administrator's Office, of course, welcomed this unexpected reinforcement of its jurisdictional claims. Still, more was needed than the Mayor's mandate to make these claims good. The City Administrator was therefore alert to prospects for new funds and programs being talked about by the Ford Foundation (which had been tapping various city agencies for reactions to its project ideas) and the new President's Committee on Juvenile Delinquency and Youth Crime. Thus, in 1961, the city was ripe for a bid from the Federal government. There was political pressure on the Mayor for a new approach, there was an agency in the city government whose own interest would nicely complement the Federal endeavor, and there was community readiness in the group eagerly seeking funds on the Lower East Side.

Mechanisms to Facilitate Collaboration

In 1962 the Mobilization For Youth project was officially launched with an announcement by the White House of a $13,-500,000 grant. The project's jurisdiction was a sixty-seven block area carved out of the Lower East Side, and its arsenal for delinquency prevention included an elaborate battery of programs in education and youth employment, as well as assorted services to groups and to individuals and families in the community. Some of these programs were to be staffed and managed by the new project, some were to be run in partnership with established agencies, and some were to be contracted out to existing local agencies. Several

Federal agencies, the city government, and the Ford Foundation were funding it. Columbia University was tied to it as a research partner. And representatives from Columbia, several city agencies, and local groups sat on its seventy-five member board. Thus at least a beginning had been made in the new Federal strategy of intervention and collaboration in patterns of service to the ghetto.

The coalition of organizations backing this early version of "creative federalism" reached from the Federal government to the local neighborhood and swept in both public and private groups. How was a collaboration forged from among groups with ordinarily diverse interests and outlooks?

The key ingredient was the incentive of new Federal money, matched by the eagerness of local agencies for new funds. But the national government moved gingerly; it had neither the authority nor the resources to enact a strategy for the inner city unilaterally. At the outset, different organizations in different places, already alerted by the attention given the delinquency problem by the press, civic groups, and political leaders, made their separate and competitive bids for public funds. These agencies had strong commitments to their existing approaches, commitments held fast by tradition and constituency. And so Federal money was dangled before local groups, and meted out through an elaborate process of accommodation in which programs were broadened, diffused, and altered to meet the terms of political trading.

Still, the various parties to the dealing were obviously not equal partners. As each grant was negotiated, Federal conditions were imposed, and although these conditions were often compromised subsequently, the Federal agencies continued to exert the dominant influence. Moreover, the national administration dispersed its money through mechanisms which promoted collaboration, while easing the way for Federal intervention.

Structural Mechanisms

To ensure their cooperation, the Federal government required that a structure be formed which actually incorporated the groups whose support was needed. The Mobilization project was lodged in a structure which included national, city-wide, and neighborhood groups—as multiple sponsors, as representatives on the seventy-five member board, or as partners in various program activities. The city's support meant not only the Mayor's Office and the City Administrator's, but also a number of city agencies which had to be propitiated, either because the new programs impinged on their jurisdictions or because the programs required their positive cooperation. In the local neighborhood, support was needed from the settlement houses, churches, and local political leaders whose territorial and functional jurisdictions were directly affected. All of these groups were structurally tied into the new venture.

The narrow jurisdiction of the project was another structural feature which paved the way for cooperation. The diverse groups from which commitments had to be secured were likely to be wary of intrusions on their domains. To assuage their fears, the new project was set up with narrowly designated limits. As a community development venture, it was to cover only a small area on the Lower East Side. Furthermore, it was defined as a "demonstration," and so would run for only a restricted period of time. Existing organizations were in this way reassured—any infringement on their jurisdictions was to be limited in scope, and would continue for only a limited time.

Professionalism as a Mechanism

The Federal agencies were the nexus for a new scientifically oriented professionalism which has become as important in social welfare as in other fields of national life.[13] This sort of professionalism played a key role in promoting Federal intervention and collaboration through the Mobilization project. For one thing, organizational links had to be established, and changing ideas com-

[13] The political uses of professionalism in social welfare are discussed at greater length in a paper by the author, "Professionalism as a Political Skill: The Case of a Poverty Program," *in Personnel in Anti-Poverty Programs: Implications for Social Work Education,* New York: Council on Social Work Education, 1967, pp. 37–50.

municated. In this process, the professionals associated with the university, the foundation, and the Federal bureaucracy were important agents. They gave advice as consultants, they served on advisory committees, they set fashions in ideas through the diffuse influence of their writings. These were the cosmopolitan professionals, moving easily from one organizational context to another, receiving grants even while they advised the granting agencies.

More important, these professionals formed a consensus of experts buttressing a political strategy. They lent to the new endeavor the prestige of their university associations, the authority of science, and the promise of progress through science. They were persuasive and articulate advocates of the advanced program ideas that were to take precedence over local and parochial agency practice. At the same time, the expertise employed by professionals swathed the project in an obscurity which, by preventing close scrutiny of the implications of various program activities, minimized dissension among the diverse groups in the collaboration.[14] In short, the professional experts associated with the Mobilization effort provided important political resources for the Federal venture into the cities.

Rationales as Mechanisms

The Mobilization project was to be an example of a comprehensive and coordinated approach to social welfare, a social planning approach to community development, an experiment in social engineering. Whatever one might think of the substance of these rationales, they provided several advantages in promoting collaboration.[15] Where concrete plans might have precipitated conflict among groups with diverse interests and perspectives, these generalities could be more easily accepted, accommodating the diverse

[14] For a more detailed discussion of these and other mechanisms to facilitate collaboration in federal programs, see an article by the author, "The Demonstration: A Federal Strategy for Local Change," in George Brager and Francis Purcell, eds., *Community Action Against Poverty*, New Haven: College and University Press, 1967.

[15] For a discussion of the uses of ideas in smoothing the way for political and bureaucratic action, see a paper by the author, "Dilemmas in Social Planning: A Case Inquiry," *The Social Service Review* (June 1968).

interests and perspectives of the collaborators. Perhaps the most useful rationale of all in this regard was the stress on experimentation and innovation, which served to relax the logic of any set of ideas, permitting an almost startling flexibility (as when a Ford Foundation official said, "Poverty with spirit can do tremendous things"). To call for innovation was to call for action, but precisely what kind of action seemed unimportant.

One thing that could be said of these general ideas is that they were all-embracing, and this was useful in still another way. A multifaceted and comprehensive project meant, in effect, a market basket of program activities designed to entice the different agencies whose collaboration was needed, each according to its own orientation and interest. And, all talk of comprehensiveness aside, as each group focused on the aspects of a project germane to its own interests, it had little need to examine the total set of actions contemplated by the project or to contend with the ideas which inspired those actions. For example, the staff of the City Administrator's Office saw in Mobilization an opportunity to expand their own planning functions and were quite indifferent to the youth recreation programs included as a concession to the local voluntary agencies. Ideas like "comprehensive and coordinated social planning" could sweep in these diverse activities, lending them a seeming coherence and distinction.

The Federal problem of intervention and collaboration in the cities was not solved all at once. Mobilization was only the beginning of a strategy that was developed through a continuing process of trial and error. Programs were fumbled, overreaching themselves only to be withdrawn and then put forward again with new and conciliatory elaborations. The executive directors of the early juvenile delinquency projects suffered startling occupational mortality—including in time the executive staff of Mobilization—as one after another ran afoul of city government. In the end, only a few projects survived. Conflict stemmed primarily from jurisdictional squabbles between new neighborhood agencies established with Federal funds and traditional municipal departments. The fact that these new agencies tried to serve ghetto groups by pressuring municipal agencies also did not help. And, of course, urban leaders soon realized that the new funds being channelled directly to neighborhoods could not be exploited by them for patronage and publicity. When the anti-poverty program generated a similar system of neighborhood agencies, but on a much larger scale, mayors and local bureaucrats throughout the land were outraged. The national administration subsequently retreated, conceding new administrative guidelines providing for more city control. The Model Cities program, for example, is designed to avoid some of this bruising conflict by funnelling Federal benefits to the ghetto by way of city government. Thus it wraps in local politicians, but nevertheless subjects them to the Federal requirement that they negotiate and reach accommodations with ghetto residents and leaders before funds will be allocated.

The originators of Mobilization For Youth often note proudly that Mobilization was a model for the early delinquency-prevention programs, and subsequently for other community action programs. They attribute this influence to the power of the new ideas of service that developed on the Lower East Side. Mobilization was indeed influential, but not only as a programmatic model. It was influential because it had been an opportune context in which the Federal agencies could explore new modes of intervention and collaboration in the cities. It was this political strategy which became the model for later programs.[16]

The Subordination of Social Planning

The mode of decision espoused by most welfare-oriented professionals emphasizes a comprehensive, rationalistic orientation toward policy. Public decisions should be made in terms of first

[16] Direct intervention in the ghetto is not the only Federal strategy for dealing with its political troubles in the cities. See the following articles written by the author with Richard A. Cloward: "Black Control of the Cities: Heading It Off with Metropolitan Government," *The New Republic*, Part I, September 30, 1967, and Part II, October 7, 1967; and "Ghetto Redevelopment: Corporate Imperialism for the Poor," *The Nation*, October 10, 1967.

principles of knowledge and value and should take account of all
the conditions pertinent to these first principles. Advocates of
social planning extend this ideal, believing that the diverse activities
of various agencies can presumably be coordinated in terms of
coherent and consistent interpretations of public policy issues.

But, as this history reveals, organizations enter into collaboration
in quite another way. The bases for cooperation are the interests
of the different parties rather than a comprehensive and rational-
ized scheme of action. Public policy is a bundle, bits and pieces of
which are divided and shifted about to secure the support necessary for collective action.

In its first *Report to the President,* the President's Committee
described the new Mobilization For Youth project as "the most
advanced program yet devised to combat delinquency on a broad
scale. Never before have neighborhood workers, the city government, the Federal government, private agencies and a great university of the stature of Columbia University joined together for a
planned coordinated attack on the sources of delinquency. Mobilization For Youth is the first concrete example of the comprehensive
local action we believe necessary to meet the complex problems
facing today's youth." [17] The Mobilization For Youth project was
indeed comprehensive, in the sense that an array of neighborhood,
city, and Federal agencies had been brought into collaboration. In
the process, however, a range of goals had been promulgated for
the project, and a variety of programs and structures had been incorporated. Most of the goals were very general and might be
contradictory. Moreover, the relationship of goals to concrete
programs and structures was at best unclear.[18]

[17] See *Report to The President,* transmitted by the President's Committee
on Juvenile Delinquency and Youth Crime, May 31, 1962, mimeographed.
In 1963, Congresswoman Edith Green (Democrat from Oregon) denounced
these claims as extravagant, demanding more modest and practical endeavors, much to the discomfiture of Administration officials.

[18] The planning document which described the battery of Mobilization
programs, and the structural arrangements to implement them, ran to
several hundred pages, and even so was often far from detailed. See *A
Proposal for the Prevention and Control of Delinquency by Expanding
Opportunities,* New York; Mobilization For Youth, 1961, 617 pp.

The Scientific Investigation of Social Policy

For example, one of the goals asserted for the Mobilization project, and the primary one from the perspective of its original National Institute of Mental Health sponsors was the scientific investigation of delinquency-prevention techniques. Indeed, some of the early publicity described the project as a new venture in "social engineering." According to this view, the project area was, in effect, a sixty-seven block laboratory, in which the service programs would be carried out as a series of scientific experiments.

A scientific investigation entailed several requirements, none easy to meet. It meant that the programs would be designed with reference to research surveys conducted during the earlier planning period. It also meant that the outcomes of the action programs would be carefully evaluated by scientific research. Finally, a scientific investigation meant that the overall framework for the service programs was derived from basic theoretical formulations regarding delinquency. Little of this was in fact realizable.

For research data to be useful in formulating programs, an extended wait would be required to permit an interchange between data and program designs. But most of the local organizational backers of Mobilization, as well as the practitioners hired as staff, wanted visible services, and quickly. As a result, the scheduling of research and the planning of action were contemporaneous, for otherwise the action programs (and presumably the goal of reducing delinquency) would have been considerably delayed.

Even if such a delay had been acceptable, the research could be useful in designing programs suggested by the opportunity-theory perspective only if the data gathered were pertinent to that perspective. One of the major devices used by the research team was the attitude survey, through which adolescents and adults in the community were questioned as to their opinions and perceptions on a range of items, particularly their attitudes toward delinquency and their perceptions of opportunities. Such surveys have become very popular in sociology and survey methodology has become highly refined. But the information suggested as pertinent by the opportunity-theory perspective—the distribution of employment opportunities, for example, or the existence of institutional barriers to educational achievement or to occupational mobility—could not be gathered by community attitude surveys. Although research techniques were well suited to conducting surveys, pertinent research on institutional structures was difficult to develop. No less important, as became evident when such studies were suggested, these institutions were not willing to lend themselves to research scrutiny, and the project had no means of coercing them.

Several studies were designed with the intent of evaluating program outcomes, but the rigid requirements of that kind of experimental research were in continual tension with the imperatives of providing services, and only a few of the studies were successfully completed. For example, experimental research required that control groups be set up, meaning that some people would be arbitrarily denied services and others arbitrarily selected for services. An experimental design also required that each program and its service population remain discreet: the diverse program activities were not to overlap and contaminate each other. Such restrictions seemed intolerable to practitioners who saw services as filling human needs, and who also believed in the multifaceted approach. Moreover, practitioners, particularly in a neighborhood-based project, had to concern themselves with maintaining the good will of their clientele, who could scarcely be expected to appreciate the scientific investigation of social policy as grounds for denying or limiting services.

If program outcomes were to be evaluated by research, program activities would also have to be clearly structured and stable, so that the studies were evaluating some definable method and not a fluid and changing process of uncertain character. But, practitioners could not be bound in advance, trusting as they did to their experience and art in dealing with situations which could not be fully appreciated at the outset, and, in any case, were always changing. Finally, evaluation of programs required that the intended outcomes be defined by researchable indices, preferably subject to quantifiable measurement. Most social welfare services, however, are associated with valued outcomes of a very diffuse and qualitative nature. A process of specification and quantification was likely to limit the focus to outcomes that could be clearly described and measured, and these were likely to be both different from and fewer than the outcomes considered pertinent by the practitioners.

In short, neither research interests nor research personnel were so authoritative as to structure the service programs or to force definition of their intended outcomes. Mobilization was a collaborative endeavor, backed by groups with research interests and groups with social welfare interests. Accordingly the project undertook both research and social welfare operations, blending and compromising both research and service imperatives.

Even in the abstract, however, quite apart from the limitations imposed by a project in which practitioners—and not academicians —had considerable say, the goal of a scientific experiment in social policy was formidable. The basic theory of delinquency and opportunity was far too broad and abstract to be tested by research of concrete programs. Such an extension of the theory would have been an overwhelming intellectual task. In any case, the kinds of evaluation that would be made possible by such an extension of the theory would not test theory, but only specific propositions describing the action strategies. This inherent gap between basic theory and concrete action seemed not to be recognized by the Federal agencies responsible, which were only too willing to borrow the authority of science to support their endeavors.

Such dilemmas never overwhelmed the project planners, perhaps because they were wise enough not to make too strenuous an attempt to derive program activities from statements about the goals of the project. The battery of programs was formed in quite another way—through innumerable accommodations with the different organizational partners. Even the local agencies, which were in the end only minor partners, still got their share of counseling and recreational activities. But while statements about goals did not dictate this process of accommodation, they were still useful. All of the agencies could share not only in the benefits of programs, but also in the prestige attending these lofty purposes. The local agencies, by making an early bid for funds, had brought the Federal strategy for the inner city to the Lower East Side. In this way they not only had received new program funds but also had transformed their jurisdictional terrain into a sixty-seven block laboratory in community development to prevent delinquency (and poverty) by strategies of innovation and experimentation, and by comprehensive and coordinated reorganization of social services.

Conclusion

Today many people are becoming skeptical of government social welfare programs. The critics who analyze these failures often view government social welfare programs as hamstrung by a kind of persistent incompetence, an incompetence amplified by the complexity of our contemporary social problems. Thus goals are said to be hazy and ill defined; implementing structures and programs are designed carelessly or inexpertly; and day-to-day bureaucratic operations are allowed to proceed as if on their own volition, disconnected from program and goals. It is as though the government apparatus were mired in sluggish incompetence and could be moved forward if only we mustered our full resources of intelligence.

But this perspective takes little account of the fundamental political nature of social-welfare measures—spawned primarily to maintain a political leadership, and then continuously adapted to a changing political environment. In that process of adaptation, public goals are a political resource more than a set of first principles guiding action. Goals can be formulated, broadened, diffused, and multiplied to suit political needs. Similarly, the concrete programs and structures launched under the banner of lofty public goals are in fact molded to deal with the various political circumstances of any agency and to suit the political leadership on which the agency depends. Through this process government action may become unintelligible to the critic who looks at goals and programs to discover a paradigm for rational action. But the motivating force in government action, the force which shapes public goals and the programs and structures created in their name, reflects another sort of rationalism—the adaptive rationalism through which a political system and its member parts are maintained.[19]

[19] An expanded version of this chapter appears as "Federal Intervention in The Cities: The New Urban Programs As A Political Strategy," *Handbook on The Studies of Social Problems,* Ed. Erwin O. Smigel, New York: Rand McNally, 1969. Permission to reprint the above version from Rand McNally is gratefully acknowledged.

Epilogue

Harold H. Weissman

Mobilization For Youth probably helped more people, influenced more professional thinking, and effected more social changes than any other social agency in our time. Tens of thousands of poor people on the Lower East Side were reached by the agency—children were taught to read, school dropouts were given training and jobs, dilapidated apartments were renovated, families on welfare were assisted in demanding adequate allowances, citizens were helped to register and vote, etc. A great many Mobilization staff members went on to teach in universities; professional journals abound with articles written about Mobilization and about the ideas developed at the agency. And in some measure, changes in policy and procedure in the Welfare Department, school system, and work training programs reflect the activities of Mobilization.

As with any first of its kind, a great deal of the attention that was showered on Mobilization was based on the fact of its newness. With the passage of time its limitations as well as its true significance have become clearer. A brief summation is therefore in order.

Many factors account for the agency's successes. Mobilization was fortunate in attracting an extremely able staff. In Richard Cloward, George Brager, and James McCarthy it had a unique and rare combination of theoretical sophistication, practical application, and dedication to an idea. If any one man was able to succeed them, it was Bertram Beck. Of equal import to the quality of its staff and leadership was the fact that Mobilization was based on an avowedly sociological rather than psychological theory. It stubbornly refused to be diverted from attempting to deal with the conditions that cause poverty by an overconcern with the idiosyncratic factors related to any one person's poverty, to be diverted from institutional reform because of the need for reform and change on the part of individuals enmeshed in the institutions. In effect Mobilization proclaimed that it is unrealistic to attempt to help people to change if the factors—or at least a significant part of them—which caused their difficulty in the first place are not themselves first changed.

During its first years of operation, Mobilization had a variety of objectives. It began as an attack on juvenile delinquency geared toward demonstration and research. It was also seen as an attempt to develop new service technologies in social casework, community organization, legal aid, and other areas. To the broad public it was often projected as an instrument of social reform and institutional change. As poverty was more and more defined as a major social problem, MFY's programs were increasingly oriented toward dealing with it.

These goals are quite disparate. No one agency could be expected to deal with all of them without considerable strain. Piven, Rein, and Miller have discussed in detail the problems inherent in attempting to deal with so many diverse ends in one large demonstration project: the conflict among goals, the problems in funding, and the difficulty of obtaining the resources needed to achieve goals. They have drawn heavily upon the MFY experience in developing their ideas. A major criticism of these writers is related to the scope of Mobilization-like programs:

> Even if we are ready to make the more rash assumption that such efforts represent coordination or comprehensiveness, the problem of scope remains. . . . For example, some programs, like public assistance, carry external stigma, a repressive means test, as well as low standards of subsistence. To evaluate the impact of public assistance on some dependent variable like rehabilitation, it may be

necessary to change the whole operation of welfare systems, rather than to create partial changes in selected variables within the system, such as client-worker interaction, quality of worker training, worker-client ratios. The demonstration may fail because experimentation must modify the whole rather than a fragment. Yet such failures may obscure the relevance and importance of these selected variables if they followed large-scale changes in social organization.[1]

Mobilization, in fact, did not have the scope necessary to achieve its avowed ends. By associating delinquency with conditions of economic and social deprivation, MFY accepted the need for broad social, economic, and institutional change. Obviously such an attack on delinquency and poverty requires great resources. Mobilization's resources, in the form of the opportunities it made available, were not adequate. The most significant opportunities were beyond its scope, such as an adult job and job-training program.

Another general limitation on Mobilization grew out of one of its greatest strengths—the fact that it was based on a sociological theory. Unfortunately this theory, opportunity theory, as developed in the agency's original proposal, was not fully operationalized. What is the relation between an educational opportunity and a job opportunity? Is the way an opportunity is provided as significant as the presence of the opportunity itself? Is one opportunity more important than another? Mobilization was hampered by the incomplete development of its theoretical base.[2] As such, it suffered from all the problems attendant on invention and innovation—

---

[1] Martin Rein and S. M. Miller, "The Demonstration Project as a Strategy of Change," paper presented at the Columbia University–Mobilization For Youth Training Institute Workshop, April 1964, mimeographed, p. 6; Frances Fox Piven, "The Demonstration Project: A Federal Strategy for Local Change," (mimeographed, New York, Mobilization For Youth, 1965).

[2] Had opportunity theory been more fully developed, policy dilemmas which the agency never adequately resolved might have been better handled: What are appropriate demands to make on clients? How can service needs be met without sacrificing the requisites of demonstration and research? With what institutions is the risk of confrontation worth taking? A failure of the research department to date is that it has not produced a comprehensive critique of opportunity theory based on the Mobilization For Youth experience.

false starts, mistakes, unanticipated events, and the like. Rein and Miller have put it as follows:

> Since urban problems indeed are interwoven, the thrust is toward multiple programs. But the use of simultaneous demonstrations—in education, employment, guidance, recreation, etc.—within a limited geographic area does not by itself assure coordinated treatment, only saturation, the layering of programs without their fusion.[3]

Mobilization's response to the lack of specificity in its theory was to attack pragmatically the problems of the neighborhood, leaning on the theory when it was helpful, ignoring it at other times, and expanding on it on others. The effects of this pragmatic approach merit some recapitulation.

Effects on Delinquency

Mobilization, as noted, was originally conceived as an effort to reduce and control the incidence of delinquency. The theoretical basis on which the agency operated asserts that it is the lack of congruence between the aspirations of youth and the opportunities open to them that in the main accounts for delinquent adaptations. In attempting to open up new opportunities through a variety of programs, MFY expanded the boundaries of its concern from delinquency to poverty, since lack of opportunity is certainly one of the preconditions of poverty as well as of delinquency. Thus the individual delinquent was never the chief focus of attention, as he would have been in a casework-oriented agency. In addition, to deal with youths apart from their families, friends, and neighborhood seemed shortsighted. Programs therefore recruited their participants and clientele not only from the adjudicated delinquent population but rather from the poor segments of the community, whether delinquent or not. The project and its programs were aimed at the *conditions* which promoted delinquency. This was clearly a long-range strategy, not easily evaluated in the short run.

[3] Rein and Miller, *op. cit.,* p. 6.

The results achieved by MFY in following this theoretical approach are difficult to evaluate for other reasons as well. First, many events occurred during the project's life which were out of MFY's control and which had significant effects on the neighborhood and its residents. The foremost of these were the civil-rights movement and the War on Poverty. Second, the agency did not have the scope or the resources to affect the conditions of poverty on the Lower East Side.[4]

In effect, opportunity theory was never really tested. Third, any analysis of impact is affected by mobility in and out of the neighborhood. Approximately one out of every four residents of the MFY area moves at least once a year. The population was forever changing.

The following statistics may be useful in evaluating MFY's success with delinquent-prone youth aged sixteen to twenty.

	Total *Lower East Side*		*MFY* *Serviced Areas*		*Non-MFY* *Serviced Areas*	
	1962	*1966*	*1962*	*1966*	*1962*	*1966*
Juvenile arrests	1,011	1,153	603	737	408	416
Delinquent rate per 1,000 youths	94.1	105	97.3	115.7	89.9	91.7

While on the surface these figures show a higher percentage increase in delinquency in the MFY serviced areas, there are compelling reasons to believe that the results are just the opposite. For both 1962 and 1966, percentage rates of offenses per thousand population are based on 1960 census figures. In fact, from 1960 to 1966 several public-housing projects opened up in the MFY serviced area, displacing large numbers of older people and substantially increasing the number of youths in the area. Thus, while

[4] As noted, the failure of MFY to include an adult employment program was the most glaring limitation in scope, one which it shared with the whole War on Poverty.

the number of arrests undoubtedly increased, the rate of arrests per thousand in all likelihood decreased. The non-MFY serviced area has had no appreciable change in youth population from 1960 to 1967. An estimate of an increase of 1,500 youths in the MFY area by 1966 shows a decrease in delinquency.[5]

	MFY Serviced Area		Non-MFY Serviced Area	
	1962	1966	1962	1966
Juvenile arrests	603	737	408	416
Delinquency rate per 1,000 youths	97.3	90.6	89.9	91.7

In MFY's efforts to cope with delinquency, a number of valuable program innovations were developed—adolescent service centers, work crews, cultural arts, etc. But the hope never materialized that Mobilization would coordinate the efforts of all local social agencies to help individual delinquents. This occurred partly because MFY —more than the local agencies—was more interested in dealing with the causes of delinquency than with individual delinquents,[6] in part to the local agencies' reluctance to be coordinated, and in part to the lack of agreement on how best to coordinate services.[7]

[5] MFY of course selected as its target area one which would have a very high delinquency rate. What was not realized at first was that the area chosen also had the highest rate of movement in and out. Such factors as mobility, inadequate census data, and changing police methods and deployment of personnel, raise doubts as to the validity of juvenile delinquency statistics. The above estimate is admittedly rough and does not take into account the fact that the eleven-to-fifteen age group in 1960 was considerably larger than the sixteen-to-twenty age group at that time. The natural increases in the sixteen-to-twenty group by 1966 are assumed to be constant in both MFY and non-MFY serviced areas and were not figured in the above estimate. Such increases would decrease the delinquency rates in both areas.

[6] MFY did not seriously attempt to integrate all of its services on behalf of individual delinquents. A client might partake of one or a variety of services, depending considerably on his own wishes, rather than be subjected to a prescribed sequence of services. As such Mobilization was not really a controlled delinquency experiment.

[7] The director of the Division of Employment Opportunities tended to view work training as the core of the agency with all other services being

What Mobilization did achieve was to expose the fact that institutions geared to serving the delinquent were not doing so effectively—the schools, the courts, the job-training programs. Even though its original Proposal suggested that delinquency could be cured by professional interventions of teachers, social workers, vocational counselors, its actions spoke otherwise. Rather than let professionals become a buffer between delinquents and society, Mobilization suggested that such professionals and the institutions which they serve must be watched by the public and that this surveillance is best carried out by the consumers as well as the providers of the institutional service.

Effects on the Social Professions

While it is difficult to substantiate the effect MFY had on delinquency and poverty, there can be little doubt that the agency had an overwhelming influence on the practice of social work, law, and vocational education. By the start of the 1960's, social welfare had realized that by and large its private agencies had disengaged themselves from serving the poor. MFY increasingly showed that this segment of the population could be reached by a social agency. A careful study of MFY's records for the first three years of its operation concluded: "In its first three years, MFY reached disproportionately large numbers of youngsters under twenty, Negroes and Puerto Ricans, members of broken homes, families on welfare and large families." [8] It also provided a staggering amount of help—educational, legal, employment, etc.

To reach the previously unreachable, the agency developed a variety of innovative program structures and techniques, many of which have since been adopted by other agencies and institutions.

---

coordinated around it, the director of Community Development felt similarly about community organization as did the director of Services to Individuals and Families, etc. In part this was caused by the incomplete development of opportunity theory.

[8] Steven J. Leeds, *Who Was Reached?* (New York, Columbia University School of Social Work, Research Center, 1967), p. 9. This report gives a program-by-program analysis of participants.

The concept of the social worker as advocate has already had profound effects on the field. Neighborhood service centers have spread throughout the country. The first welfare-client organizations were developed at MFY and from them has grown a whole national movement. The community-action section of the Economic Opportunity Act, which launched the War on Poverty, was in the main modeled after the MFY experience. The national Neighborhood Youth Corps was predated by MFY's own Urban Youth Work Corps. The agency pioneered in the use of local residents as service workers. Many of the ideas behind the movement for new careers for the poor were tried out and developed at MFY. This volume has documented the pioneering efforts of MFY's Legal Services. Other volumes have detailed such innovations as the cultural-arts program, which presaged the current emphasis on "black is beautiful," the adolescent service centers, the Homework Helper Program, the food co-ops, etc. If program innovation is a valid criterion for MFY's efforts, then the agency can be judged as overwhelmingly successful.[9]

Effects on Public Institutions

The primary impetus behind many of MFY's innovations was the agency's desire to bring about changes in public institutions that serve the poor. When it became obvious through work with individual clients that the Welfare Department, the courts, the school system, and the housing departments were not operating effectively, the agency consciously set out to confront these public institutions with their inadequacies.[10]

It is clear that institutions are not solely to blame for the prob-

[9] Staff delivered hundreds of speeches and wrote scores of professional papers. A partial list of these papers is found in *Master Annotated Bibliography* (New York, Mobilization For Youth, 1965).

[10] Several of the papers in these volumes discuss the problems inherent in a situation when a social agency confronts a public institution. See in particular the chapter on "Educational Innovation: The Case of an External Innovating Organization," in Vol. 3, *Employment and Educational Services*.

lems and predicaments of their clients; the Welfare Department is not the cause of people being on welfare, nor is the school system completely at fault for the inability of children to learn to read. But it is reasonable to expect that these institutions will operate so as not to frustrate attempts to help individuals deal with their problems. Mobilization exposed the institutional cellars where the poor come for their education, their justice, their jobs. While it is a truism that institutions are slow to change, MFY showed how social agencies could assist this process of change. It helped force the Welfare Department of New York City to adjust to the demands of welfare clients. It demonstrated how legal services for the poor can contribute in changing institutions.

The current battle over the decentralization of schools in New York was predated by Mobilization Of Mothers. Most important, MFY helped to establish the principle that public institutions must be held accountable to the public, and that some measure of that accountability must be to the clients that they serve. The poor were given a voice.

Community action, the attempt to organize low-income communities to protest and demand change, was extremely important as a spur to social reform. Its basic strategy was to bring small resources to bear at key leverage points in society in order that larger resources would be made available. It was hoped that through community-action efforts the political power of the poor would be organized and would force social institutions and ultimately political parties to accommodate to the demands of the poor.

It has become clear that this strategy has certain limitations. First, the poor compromise many different groups, whose needs are not altogether congruent; political organization is therefore difficult. Welfare-client groups including many Puerto Ricans were booed by other Puerto Ricans when they marched in a Puerto Rican Day parade. In New York Negroes and Puerto Ricans are constantly battling for jobs and control of the poverty program. Second, outside resources of money and organizational skill are needed if the poor are to be organized. It is clear at this point that these resources are not forthcoming from public funds in the amounts needed. Third, community action has tended to focus first on gaining power for the poor—power to control local schools, to influence the policies of the Welfare Department, and then ultimately sufficient power to have their economic demands met. The strategy assumes that the poor themselves desire power and will enlist in efforts to gain it. In fact the poor man is much more concerned about money and purchasing power than he is in wielding power over malfunctioning social institutions. His interest in community action is therefore episodic, related to the short-run prospects of immediate gain, and unsuited to a long-range strategy of developing a political power base.[11] The only really successful community-action campaign at MFY was related to welfare, and money was a central factor in this campaign.

Community action in the original MFY Proposal was concerned with the ability of low-income communities to solve their own problems. Shortly after the inception of the project it was realized that such communities need power to achieve these ends. Experience casts considerable doubt whether community action alone can develop such power, especially since in our society power is considerably grounded on an economic base. In all likelihood, community action needs to address itself to more limited ends, economic opportunities being one, than securing diffuse political power for the poor. Probably the opportunity structure must be altered if the power structure is to be measurably changed.[12]

Effects on Poverty

The best-informed judgment at MFY is that, if poverty is to be eradicated, then the economic problems of the poor must take precedence over their social and political problems.[13] While the

11 After five years of MFY's efforts in community action, relatively few leaders emerged from the local population.

12 This issue is discussed in more detail in the paper "Social Action in a Social Work Context" in Vol. 2, *Community Development*.

13 This does not mean that "psychic income," or those constellations of feelings and attitudes about self that adhere to individuals from their status in society, can be ignored. For an analysis of the conceptual problems involved in the War on Poverty, and the reasons why agencies like Mobiliza-

various problems that beset the slum are intertwined with and affect one another, it is likely that these problems are not equally important.

Experience in a variety of MFY's programs suggests the centrality of economic factors; people who are employed are more likely to register and to vote after registration. The more stable a family's employment and income, the more likely its members are to take part in social-action campaigns. The more closely remedial-education classes are related to employment, the more people attend them. The more recent one's last job, the more likely one is to be actively looking for a job. Mickens has stated this point of view as regards employment:

> The failure to come to grips with chronic urban unemployment and underemployment probably devalues whatever gains are scored in other areas of social action. No amount of discussion on "tangles of pathology" should becloud this point. Since employment problems are the leading links in the tangle, gains in this area produce large spillover benefits all along the chain and failures undercut gains scored elsewhere. Granted that the vicious tangle of poverty represents a total self-reinforcing system, such that every community problem generates heightened individual and family problems which further exacerbate the community condition, it does not follow that each community problem must be simultaneously taken in tow by action on all fronts.[14]

Poverty is a condition in which an individual does not have enough money to purchase the goods and services that he needs. If this situation is to be overcome, then the slum neighborhood needs an institution that concerns itself with the economic problems of the area. At this point, few if any slums have such an agency. The major task of Mobilization during the next years of its operation is

tion, given their present structure and program, cannot eradicate poverty, see Daniel P. Moynihan, "The Professors and the Poor," *Commentary* (August 1968).

[14] Alvin Mickens, *Manpower Perspectives for Urban Development* (New York, New York University Center for the Study of Unemployed Youth, 1967), p. 14.

to transform itself into an institution which translates its concern for the social and emotional problems of people into economic activities.[15] In so doing the agency remains true to its basic premise that social services are not enough.

Summation

One final word deserves to be said about the people who worked at MFY. Though many were bright, gifted, and extremely dedicated, not all were so exceptional. One would expect as much in an agency which over the years employed well over 1,000 people. Yet the combined effort of the staff, the concerns, the hopes, the joys, even the frustration cannot help but make one feel that poverty and ignorance will ultimately be overcome. If Mobilization did not provide all the answers, it surely sustained a spirit for those who will take up the cause in the future. For this, we are proud.

[15] For a preliminary discussion of the techniques and programs by which MFY hopes to achieve its economic goals, see Harold H. Weissman, "The Economic Development of the Inner City," *Social Work Practice* (New York, Columbia University Press, 1968).

Appendices

1. Index of Research Studies [1]

Juvenile Delinquency: Its Causes and Prevention

Richard A. Cloward "Illegitimate Means, Anomie, and Deviant Behavior," *American Sociological Review,* Vol. 24, No. 2 (April 1959), pp. 164–76. (The forerunner of the theory on which MFY was based.)

> Expanded and applied specifically to explain varying forms of gang delinquency in Chapters 6, 7, and 8 of *Delinquency and Opportunity* (see below).
>
> > See also, Robert K. Merton, "Social Conformity, Deviation and Opportunity Structures: A Comment on the Contributions of Dubin and Cloward," *American Sociological Review,* Vol. 24, No. 2 (April 1959) pp. 177–89.

Richard A. Cloward and Lloyd E. Ohlin *Delinquency and Opportunity: A Theory of Delinquent Gangs,* Glencoe, Illinois, The Free Press, 1960, 220 pp. (The theory on which MFY was based.)

> This book received the Dennis Carroll Award of the International Society of Criminology in 1965. The award, given in the name of the founder and first president of the society, is made once every five years upon the recommendation of an international jury of scholars.
>
> Article-length critiques of *Delinquency and Opportunity* can be found as follows:

---

[1] Only retrievable published material is included in this bibliography. For an analysis of the problems of mounting research at Mobilization see "Politics and Planning: Mobilization as a Model" in this volume.

1. Jackson Toby, " 'Delinquency and Opportunity': Review Article," *British Journal of Sociology,* Vol. 12 (September 1961), pp. 282–89.

2. Donald Cook, "Delinquency and the Goods of the World," *New Republic,* April 24, 1961, pp. 21–24.

3. John Kitsuse, "Review of 'Delinquency and Opportunity'," *The Sociological Quarterly,* Vol. 2 (July 1961), pp. 222–24.

4. Clarence Schrag, " 'Delinquency and Opportunity': Review Article," *Sociology and Social Research,* Vol. 46 (January 1962), pp. 167–75.

5. Irwin Deutscher, "Continuity in Sociological Theory: Some Critical Comments on Cloward and Ohlin's 'Delinquency and Opportunity'," *The Journal of Educational Sociology* (March 1963).

6. Jerome Himelhoch, " 'Delinquency and Opportunity': An End and a Beginning of Theory," in Alvin W. Gouldner and S. M. Miller, editors, *Applied Sociology,* New York, The Free Press of Glencoe, 1965, pp. 189–206.

Richard A. Cloward   "Social Problems, Social Definitions, and Social Opportunities," keynote paper, *Proceedings, Seminar on Social Forces and Juvenile Delinquency,* New York, National Council on Crime and Delinquency, March, 1964, pp. 1–44.

In the following research conducted by Paul Lerman, the elements of several theories of delinquency—including *Delinquency and Opportunity*—were systematically tested.

Paul Lerman   *Issues in Subcultural Delinquency,* unpublished doctoral dissertation, Columbia University, 1966.

———   "Argot, Symbolic Deviance, and Subcultural Delinquency," *American Sociological Review,* Vol. 32, No. 2 (April 1967), pp. 209–24.

———   "Gangs, Networks, and Subcultural Delinquency," *American Journal of Sociology,* Vol. 73, No. 1 (July 1967), pp. 63–72.

———   "Individual Values, Peer Values, and Subcultural Delinquency," *American Sociological Review,* Vol. 33, No. 2 (April 1968), pp. 219–35.

Services To Individuals and Families

The following articles describe and document the general movement in private agencies away from serving the poor.

Richard A. Cloward   "Social Class and Private Social Agencies," *11th Proceedings,* Council on Social Work Education, 1963, pp. 123–37.

Richard A. Cloward and Irwin Epstein   "Private Social Welfare's Disengagement from the Poor: The Case of Family Adjustment Agencies," *Proceedings, Eighth Annual Social Work Day Conference,* State University of New York at Buffalo, May 12, 1965, pp. 1–54.

The following articles, based on observation of MFY's storefront casework offices, suggest forms of service most helpful to the poor.

Richard A. Cloward and Richard M. Elman   "Poverty, Injustice and the Welfare State," *The Nation:*
Part 1: "An Ombudsman for the Poor?" February 28, 1966, pp. 230–34.
Part 2: "How Rights Can Be Secured," March 7, 1966, pp. 264–68.
Both parts reprinted in Louis A. Ferman, Joyce L. Kornbluh, and Alan Haber, editors, *Poverty in America,* revised edition, Ann Arbor, Michigan, University of Michigan Press, 1968, pp. 322–30.

Richard A. Cloward and Richard M. Elman   "Advocacy in the Ghetto," *Transaction,* December, 1966.

Richard A. Cloward and Richard M. Elman   "The Storefront on Stanton Street: Advocacy in the Ghetto," in George A. Brager and Francis P. Purcell, editors, *Community Action Against Poverty,* New Haven, College and University Press, 1967, pp. 253–82.

Richard A. Cloward   "An Ombudsman for Whom?" *Social Work,* Vol. 12, No. 2 (April 1967), pp. 117–18.

The World of Education

Richard A. Cloward and James A. Jones   "Social Class: Educational Attitudes and Participation," in A. Harry Passow, editor, *Education in Depressed Areas,* New York, Teacher's College Bu-

reau of Publications, 1963, pp. 190–216. (A review of attitudes
toward education based on data gathered in a survey of residents
in the MFY area.)

John A. Michael "On Neighborhood Context and College Plans,"
American Sociological Review, Vol. 31 (October 1966), pp.
702–06.

John A. Michael "Socialization and School Dropout: A Study of the
Intergenerational Transmission of Socioeconomic Ideas and
their Impact on Educational Attainment," unpublished doctoral
dissertation, Columbia University, 1968.

One of MFY's largest and most successful educational programs employed high-school students to tutor underachieving
third and fourth graders. The results of the program, which
was structured as a classical experimental design, are reported
as follows:

Robert D. Cloward "Studies in Tutoring," *Journal of Experimental
Education,* Fall 1967, 36:14–25.

Robert D. Cloward "The Nonprofessional in Education," *Educational
Leadership,* April 1967, 24:604–06.

Organizing the Poor

Richard A. Cloward and Frances Fox Piven "The Weight of the
Poor: A Strategy to End Poverty," *The Nation,* May 2, 1966,
pp. 510–17. (Based on MFY's experience in organizing welfare
recipients, this article set forth an organizing theory and called
for the formation of a national welfare-rights movement.)

Richard A. Cloward "Race and the City: A Strategy of Disruption,"
Center Dairy: Center for the Study of Democratic Institutions,
January–February 1967. (Some further notes on a theory of
organizing the poor.)

The following five articles recount the origins and progress
of the National Welfare Rights Movement.

Richard A. Cloward and Frances Fox Piven "Notes on the Birth of a
Movement," *Guaranteed Annual Income Newsletter,* School of
Social Service Administration, University of Chicago, No. 4,
Spring 1967.

Richard A. Cloward and Frances Fox Piven "Birth of a Movement,"
The Nation, May 8, 1967, pp. 582–88.

Richard A. Cloward and Frances Fox Piven "We've Got Rights! The No-Longer Silent Welfare Poor," *The New Republic,* August 5, 1967, pp. 23–27.

Richard A. Cloward and Frances Fox Piven "Welfare Reform: Finessing the Poor," *The Nation,* October 7, 1968, pp. 332–34.

Richard A. Cloward and Frances Fox Piven "Workers and Welfare: The Poor Against Themselves," *The Nation,* November 25, 1968, pp. 558–62.

Richard A. Cloward and Frances Fox Piven "Rent Strike: Disrupting the Slum System," *The New Republic,* December 2, 1967, pp. 11–15. (An analysis of the failure of the city-wide rent strike in 1963–64, in which MFY participated, and a theory of how rent strikes can succeed.)

Richard A. Cloward and Frances Fox Piven "Dissensus Politics: A Strategy for Winning Economic Rights," *The New Republic,* April 20, 1968, pp. 20–24. (An overall theory of organizing the poor around welfare and housing.)

The Involvement of the Poor

Richard A. Cloward "Politics, Poverty and the Involvement of the Poor," mimeographed, Columbia University School of Social Work, June 1965, 20 pp.

Charles Grosser "Perceptions of Professionals, Indigenous Workers and Lower-Class Clients," unpublished doctoral dissertation, Columbia University, 1965.

Charles Grosser "Local Residents as Mediators Between Middle-Class Professional Workers and Lower-Class Clients," *Social Service Review,* Vol. 40, No. 1 (March 1966).

Charles Grosser "Class Orientation of Indigenous Staff," in George Brager and Francis Purcell, editors, *Community Action Against Poverty,* New Haven, College and University Press, 1967.

Frances Fox Piven "Participation of Residents in Neighborhood Community Action Programs" in *Social Work,* Vol. 2, No. 1 (January 1966).

The World of Work

Richard A. Cloward and Robert Ontell "Our Illusions About Training," *American Child,* Vol. 47, No. 1 (January 1965), pp. 6–10.

(An analysis of MFY's work crew and dispersed training sites is in process.)

Studies of the Profession

Frances Fox Piven   "Professionalism as a Political Skill: The Case of a Poverty Program," *Personnel in Anti-Poverty Programs: Implications for Social Work Education,* New York, Council on Social Work Education, 1967. (An analysis, based on extensive interviews with persons associated with the founding of MFY, of the use of professional skills in the political process.)

Irwin Epstein   "Social Workers and Social Action: Attitudes Toward Social Action Strategies," *Social Work,* 13:2 (April 1968), pp. 101–08. (Following the political crisis over MFY's activities in welfare and rent strike organizing, 1,500 social workers in New York City were queried regarding their attitudes toward social action.)

Harold H. Weissman   "An Exploratory Study of a Neighborhood Council: The Application of an Exchange Concept," unpublished doctoral dissertation, Columbia University, 1966.

Abraham Alcabes   "A Study of a Community's Perception and Use of Neighborhood Centers," unpublished doctoral dissertation, Columbia University, 1967.

Stephen J. Leeds   *Who Was Reached?* New York, Columbia University School of Social Work, MFY Research and Evaluation Project, 1968.

Studies of the Political Functions of the Antipoverty Program
(and of other Federal programs for the cities)

Frances Fox Piven   The following three articles, by Frances Fox Piven, based on extensive interviews with persons associated with the founding of MFY, analyze the political functions of the antipoverty program, and provide a general theory of Federal intervention in the cities.

———   "Organizational, Professional and Citizen Collaboration in Social Policy," in Erwin Smigel, editor, *Handbook on the Study of Social Problems,* New York, Rand McNally and Company, forthcoming.

———— "Some Dilemmas in Social Planning: A Case Inquiry," *Social Service Review*, June 1968.

———— "The Demonstration: A Federal Strategy for Local Change" in George Brager and Francis Purcell, editors, *Community Action Against Poverty*, New Haven, College and University Press, 1967.

Richard A. Cloward and Frances Fox Piven   "The Professional Bureaucracies: Benefit Systems as Influence Systems," in Murray Silberman, editor, *The Role of Government in Promoting Social Change*, New York, Columbia University School of Social Work, July 1966.

Richard A. Cloward and Frances Fox Piven   "Urban Disruption and the Consolidation of National Power," *Urban Riots: Violence and Social Change*, The Proceedings of the Academy of Political Science, Vol. 29, No. 1 (August 1968).

The Crisis Over Mobilization For Youth

A compilation of newspaper accounts, reports of official investigations, and other documents in connection with the political controversy over Mobilization For Youth. These volumes are only available in the libraries of leading schools of social work throughout the country.

Mobilization For Youth, The Crisis: A Documentary Record

Vol. 1. Antecedents, and August–September 1964
Vol. 2. October–November 1964
Vol. 3. January–June 1965
Vol. 4. July 1965–March 1966
Vol. 5. Miscellaneous Documents
Vol. 6. Reports of Official Investigations

Studies of Poverty, Economic and Physical Segregation, Housing and Public Welfare.

Sherman Barr   "Poverty on the Lower East Side: A View from the Bottom," *Public Welfare*, October 1965.

Sherman Barr and George A. Brager   "Perceptions and Reality: The

Poor Man's View of Social Services," in George A. Brager and Francis P. Purcell, editors, *Community Action Against Poverty,* New Haven, College and University Press, 1967.

Nathan Kantrowitz and Donnell M. Pappenfort *1960 Fact Book for the New York–Northeastern New Jersey Standard Consolidated Area: The Nonwhite, Puerto Rican, and White Non-Puerto Rican Populations,* Social Statistics for Metropolitan New York, No. 2, published jointly by Columbia, Fordham, and New York Universities, March 1966.

The following articles by Nathan Kantrowitz are based on extensive demographic studies of the New York Metropolitan area.

"Social Mobility of Puerto Ricans: Education, Occupation, and Income Changes Among Children of Migrants, New York, 1950–1960," *International Migration Review,* Vol. 2, No. 2 (Spring 1968), p. 53–72.

New York's Negro and Puerto Rican Populations in the Twentieth Century: A Study in Urban Cartography, New York, American Geographical Society, forthcoming.

"Ethnic and Racial Segregation in the New York Metropolis, 1960," *American Journal of Sociology,* May 1969.

"Estimated Net Migration And Natural Increase Component Of Population Change by Race And Ethnicity," *New York Statistician,* February 1969.

Richard A. Cloward and Frances Fox Piven "Keeping People Poor: An Essay on the Public Welfare System," in Mathew Ahmannd and Margaret Roach, editors, *The Church and the Urban Crisis,* Techny, Illinois, National Catholic Conference for Interracial Justice, Divine Word Publications, 1967, pp. 169–92.

Richard A. Cloward and Frances Fox Piven "Migration, Politics, and Welfare," *Saturday Review,* November 16, 1968, pp. 31–35.

Frances Fox Piven and Richard A. Cloward "Desegregated Housing: Who Pays for the Reformers' Ideal?," *The New Republic,* December 17, 1966, pp. 17–22.

Frances Fox Piven and Richard A. Cloward "The Case Against Urban Desegregation," *Social Work,* Vol. 12, No. 1 (January 1967), pp. 12–21.

See also Clarence Funnye and Ronald Shiffman, "The Imperative of Deghettoization: An Answer to Piven and

Cloward," *Social Work,* Vol. 12, No. 2 (April 1967), pp. 5–11; and the rejoinder by Piven and Cloward, Vol. 12, No. 3 (July 1967), pp. 110–11.

See also the response of Whitney Young, Jr., to this debate, "The Case for Urban Integration," *Ibid.,* Vol. 12, No. 3 (July 1967), pp. 12–17.

Richard A. Cloward and Frances Fox Piven   "Ghetto Redevelopment: Corporate Imperialism for the Poor," *The Nation,* October 16, 1967, pp. 365–67.

MEMBERS WHO SERVED ON
THE BOARD OF DIRECTORS
MOBILIZATION FOR YOUTH, INC.
1960–1969

Alexander J. Allen
Humberto Aponte
Hon. Abraham Beame
Florence S. Becker
Virginia Bellsmith
Louis Berkowitz
Herbert Bienstock
Eleanor L. Blum
Paul Bonynge
Dr. Howard J. Brown
Winslow Carlton
Arthur Cohn
Charles Cook
James A. Curran
P. Frederick DelliQuadri
Felix Drevon
Hon. Edward R. Dudley
Hon. James R. Dumpson
Gerald Eisner
Joseph Erazo, Esq.
Pedro Escalera
Sarah Farley
Bernard C. Fisher
Gladys Flores
Dora Gellerman
Hon. Mitchell Ginsberg
Esther Gollobin
Dr. Calvin Gross
Hon. Elinor Guggenheimer
Helen Hall
Ethan Allen Hitchcock, Esq.
William Huggins
Lesley Jackson
George James

Howard G. Janover
Madison Jones
Shirley Jones
Dr. David I. Kaplan
Hon. Florence M. Kelley
Msgr. Thomas J. Keogh
Barbara Killingsworth
Col. Herbert George King
Whitman Knapp, Esq.
Sam Kovenetsky
Hon. Anna M. Kross
Hon. Theodore H. Lang
Martin A. Livenstein
Austin H. MacCormick
Thomas McKenna
Gloria Martinez
Arthur Miller
Dr. Irving Miller
Rose Miller
Walter A. Miller
Hon. Joseph Monserrat
Wanda Moore
Catherine M. Morrow
Hon. Newbold Morris
Robert H. Mulreany
Michael J. Murphy
Hon. John Murtaugh
Rev. C. Kilmer Myers
Dr. John Niemeyer
Rabbi Seymour Nulman
Rev. Francis X. O'Brien, S.J.
Paul O'Keefe
Andrew Oliver
Haydee Ortiz

Monrad Paulsen, Esq.
Hon. Marvin E. Perkins
Morton Pepper, Esq.
Lydia Perez
Richard D. Peters
Rose Porter
Lillian Quinones
Rev. William W. Reed
Hon. William Reid
Victor Remer
Lillie Mae Robinson
Hon. Arthur J. Rogers
Julius Rothman
Ruby Russell
Richard Sachs
Leonard H. Sandler, Esq.
Petra Santiago
Dr. Eleanor B. Sheldon
Lucrecia Siatwinski
Hon. Simon Silver

Robert Simons
Dr. Simon Slavin
Norine Slaughter
Dr. John W. Slawson
Dr. Herman D. Stein
Dora Tannenbaum
Charles Tenney
Rafael Valdivieso
Stephen C. Vladeck, Esq.
George von Hilsheimer
Hon. Robert F. Wagner
Bess Miller Walsh
Lillian Weinfeld
Joseph J. Weiser, Esq.
Geoffrey R. Wiener
Dorothy Wills
Ruth Winds
Robert Wolf
Whitney Young
Rev. George D. Younger

Index